For the
Love
of
Money

✿ A MEMOIR ✿

Sam Polk

SCRIBNER
New York   London   Toronto   Sydney   New Delhi

SCRIBNER
An Imprint of Simon & Schuster, Inc.
1230 Avenue of the Americas
New York, NY 10020

First Scribner hardcover edition July 2016

SCRIBNER and design are registered trademarks of
The Gale Group, Inc., used under license by Simon & Schuster, Inc.,
the publisher of this work.

For information about special discounts for bulk purchases,
please contact Simon & Schuster Special Sales at 1-866-506-1949
or business@simonandschuster.com.

The Simon & Schuster Speakers Bureau can bring authors
to your live event. For more information or to book an event,
contact the Simon & Schuster Speakers Bureau at 1-866-248-3049
or visit our website at www.simonspeakers.com.

Interior design by Kyle Kabel

Manufactured in the United States of America

3   5   7   9   10   8   6   4   2

Library of Congress Cataloging-in-Publication Data

Polk, Sam.
For the love of money : a memoir / Sam Polk.
pages cm
1. Polk, Sam. 2. Investment advisors—United States—Biography.
3. Stockbrokers—United States—Biography. I. Title.
HG4928.5.P65A3 2015
332.6092—dc23
[B]
2015023618

ISBN 978-1-4767-8598-1
ISBN 978-1-4767-8600-1 (ebook)

To my wife and daughter

"And so we beat on, boats against the current, borne ceaselessly into the past."

—F. Scott Fitzgerald,
The Great Gatsby

"There are a thousand hacking at the branches of evil to one who is striking at the root."

—Henry David Thoreau

Contents

◻

Contents

Author's Note

◻

The events in this book are real. I've changed most names and altered some details to honor people's privacy.

Prologue

◻

The e-mail from Sean popped up in my in-box.

Come to my office.

I felt a jolt of adrenaline. It wasn't fear, exactly. It was just that so much could happen in a late-January conversation with your boss. On Wall Street, everything important—bonuses, promotions, firings—happens in January.

I leaned back in my chair and looked down the row to Sean's glass-walled office. He sat at his desk, typing on the keyboard. I could usually sense his mood from the set of his jaw, the hunch of his shoulders. Today I couldn't tell. Sean was the head of trading at Pateras Capital, one of the largest hedge funds in the world. It was rumored that in bad years he made $20 million.

I was one of five senior traders at Pateras. Each of us was responsible for a particular market. I traded bonds of companies in or near bankruptcy. The "distressed" market. The term *distressed* captured how I was feeling about my entire life.

When Sean offered me a million dollars to leave Bank of America and come to Pateras, I'd felt like I won the lottery. Pateras was one of the most prestigious hedge funds on Wall

Street. I couldn't have dreamt up a more perfect job. But in the two years since I'd arrived, I'd started to see things—about Wall Street, about myself—that I hadn't seen before. Now I wasn't even sure I wanted to be here anymore.

I typed out a reply to Sean. *Be there in two minutes.* I wanted him to think I was busy, and I also wanted to collect myself. I had some internal tension when it came to Sean.

In my first few months at Pateras I'd seen firsthand what an amazing trader Sean was. His market knowledge was encyclopedic; his instincts were fighter-pilot sharp. I started to fantasize about becoming his protégé.

But our relationship hadn't developed as I'd hoped. While Sean treated me with respect, he never focused special attention on me. He saved that for another senior trader, Derek Mabry. Derek wore expensive suits, dated models, and spent weekends in the Hamptons. Sean preferred him. When I'd see Derek sprawled on the chair in Sean's glass-walled office, embers of jealousy smoldered inside me.

I worried my big mouth had gotten me in trouble. A few times I'd been on the phone with my identical twin brother, discussing the pros and cons of leaving Wall Street, when I suddenly realized how loudly I'd been talking, and how quiet the trading floor was. I worried Sean had overheard me, that my loose lips had jeopardized my bonus. Why pay someone millions of dollars if their heart isn't in it anymore?

Sean looked up as I pulled the door open.

"How's the market?" he asked.

"Stable," I said. "Not much going on."

For the past year and a half, the market had fluctuated like a pitching boat. We were still climbing out of the Great Recession. But that day the market was quiet, as if it were taking a collective, exhausted breath.

Sean nodded. The stress of the past few years had taken its toll. He'd always been thin, but he was starting to resemble a cadaver. His head seemed enormous atop his emaciated body. You could see the shape of his skull.

"Let me get right to it," he said.

I held my breath.

"What are you expecting this year for a bonus? Give me the number," he asked.

I exhaled. We were having The Bonus Talk. I was safe, not fired. Under Sean's gaze, I searched for a response. But the answer seemed hazy, far away.

It wasn't that I hadn't thought about it. It's impossible to overstate how often Wall Street traders think about their bonuses. Those thoughts drive every trade, meeting, client dinner, and ball game. The carrot at the end of the stick.

One of the reasons you think so much about it is because you don't have much control over it. It's a great paradox on Wall Street, where you supposedly "eat what you kill," that your bonus is entirely at your boss's discretion. The more trading profits you make, the bigger your bonus will likely be. But there are other variables—how profitable the firm is, seniority, what competitors are paying. You just don't know.

It was especially true for me that year. I'd had the best trading year of my life. I'd been positioned perfectly for a market collapse. When the crash came, I'd closed out trades for huge profits, and then bought a ton of deeply distressed bonds for cents on the dollar, just as the market bottomed out. Those bonds screamed higher, and by the end of the year, I'd earned several hundred million dollars for Pateras. The year before I'd made less than half of this year's take for Pateras, and my bonus had been $1.3 million. Sean said that the longer I was at Pateras, the higher my percentage payout would be. Given how much I was up this year, a higher-percentage payout would mean a massive amount of money. NBA all-star money.

I was thirty years old. I'd been an English major. I'd managed to keep my past a secret.

I gazed back at Sean. He was about to tell me I'd make more that year than my mom, a nurse-practitioner midwife, had earned in her entire life.

"So tell me," said Sean. "What's the number?"

"I have no idea," I said.

"Your bonus this year," he said, "will be three point six million."

I took a step back, staggered. Lots of people on Wall Street make a million bucks a year. Few make almost four. It was an instant entrance into the ranks of the super wealthy. I'd yearned for this moment my whole life. And now that it had happened—now that Sean had said the actual number—I wanted more.

As I ran the numbers in my head, a hollow feeling crept into my stomach.

"So you all are paying me less of a percentage than last year?" I asked.

"I think they should have paid you more," Sean said. "But you know how Peter is." Peter Conroy, co–managing partner of Pateras, controlled the purse strings and seemed to think everyone should just be grateful to be there.

My happiness disappeared under a flash flood of anger.

"You said my percentage payout would go up," I said.

"I know," Sean said. "You need to be patient. Just look at Derek—it took him a few years, but now he's making real money." The flash flood lurched up like a wave about to break. *Derek* was making real money this year? More than me.

"This is bullshit," I said. My hands were shaking.

That night I lay in bed next to my girlfriend, Kirsten, listening to the creaks and groans of the old brownstone in Brooklyn Heights where I rented a floor. Thoughts raced through my head like motorcycles.

The image of Derek bragging about his windfall to his popped-collar Hamptons buddies made me nauseous. But what really hurt was that Sean hadn't stood up for me. He could have convinced Peter to increase my bonus, or even shaved a few million off his own for me.

But he didn't.

My face was tight with anger. But I could feel tears lying in wait, ready to stream down my cheeks.

I wasn't going to fall asleep. I knew my shifting would eventually wake Kirsten, so I sat gently up in bed, my left side suddenly cold without her next to me. I stuck my feet into my slippers and padded into the kitchen for a glass of water. I took it to the living room and sat down in the big gray chair where I usually did my reading. But instead of pulling out the worn copy of *The Great Gatsby* I was rereading, I just sat and thought about my life.

Yesterday I'd been planning to leave Wall Street; today I was devastated because my enormous bonus wasn't bigger.

What was wrong with me? How had I become like this?

CHAPTER I

Unconscious Inheritance

◻

I grew up in the suburbs around Los Angeles, in a three-bedroom house at the end of a cul-de-sac. There was a yard out front and rolling hills out back. From the outside, our house looked pretty normal. We'd moved to Los Angeles so Dad could become a screenwriter. He enrolled in film school; Mom supported the family on her nurse-practitioner salary.

They were constantly stressed about money, but Dad was always talking about how one day he'd score big. His face lit up when he talked about that future windfall, how in a single instant all our worries would disappear. I reveled in his fantasy. When a neighbor asked me that year what I wanted to be when I grew up, I smiled and answered, "Rich." Dad beamed.

I shared a bedroom with my identical twin brother. Ben and I had been through everything together—birth, potty training, first day of school. We shared clothes, a dresser, a Nintendo. Sometimes we used each other's toothbrushes. But when we were eight, I begged for a dog, and Ben seemed indifferent. So when my mom brought OJ home from a shelter and Dad, after arguing against it, finally allowed him to stay, OJ was mine.

"This dog is your responsibility," said Dad. "Not mine."

OJ was a fat little golden retriever, a Chicken McNugget

with legs. His tail never stopped wagging, and his bark was warm. I petted him incessantly, took him for three or four walks a day. I'd snap on OJ's red leash and get yanked proudly up and down our cul-de-sac.

At the end of our street sat an open lot, dusty and speckled with crabgrass. At the back of the lot a line of trees opened to a dirt path that led to the hills. The steep path wound through a thicket to a rocky clearing that looked like a moonscape, and ended in a cliff that overlooked our block. OJ and I spent hours up there.

I tried to train OJ.

"Sit," I said, standing facing him. He looked up and wagged his tail.

"Sit," I said again and pushed his bottom down. He licked my face. As soon as I let go, he was up again, rolling his head side to side and rubbing up against me. He seemed to be laughing, so I laughed. After awhile I gave up and threw the tennis ball I'd brought.

"Fetch," I said, and he scrambled off across the craggy rocks. I was careful not to throw the ball too near the cliff.

We went up there every day. After we finished playing, I'd get as close to the edge as I could. OJ would sit with his head in my lap. We'd watch the cars coming home, the lights blinking on and off, and I'd thrill in bearing secret witness to people's lives.

"Good dog," I'd say. "You are such a good dog."

I liked being out of the house, because things had recently become tense at home. Mom and Dad had started retreating into hushed conversations.

Mom had undergone a battery of tests for what she thought was a urinary tract infection. One day the hospital called with the results. They told her she had chlamydia.

"It must be a mistake," Mom said. She was married. The nurse suggested she might speak to her husband about that.

Mom was incensed. Dad, too, was appalled at that nurse but said Mom should take the medication just to be safe. He'd get tested as a precaution. A week later he told Mom that his results had come back clean. They wrote it off as a mix-up.

A few months later, Mom became pregnant with my younger brother, Daniel. Her pregnancy was a problem for my dad. Mom worked full-time, while Dad stayed home, smoked weed, and worked on a screenplay. She told him he would need to find an income-generating job.

But Dad had big aspirations for that screenplay, and was furious at Mom for getting in the way of his dreams. He started singing the Rolling Stones lyrics "I'll never be your beast of burden" when Mom was around, and muttering "cunt" when she'd storm away.

Dad found a job selling kitchen cabinets. After Daniel was born, Mom returned to working full-time, so they hired a Guatemalan woman to care for the baby. She cleaned up some during the day, but by the time Dad and Mom got home from work, the house was a mess. And on the weekends, when the housekeeper-nanny was away, the house looked like a bomb had gone off. Clothes, toys, old newspapers, and empty bowls of cereal were strewn about. The carpet in front of the TV was threadbare and covered with stains, because Ben and I ate most of our meals there.

Dad started working most weekends, and on those days Mom would retreat to her room for an afternoon nap. When I'd shake her awake for dinner, next to her would be an empty bowl with a spoon stuck in the hardened residue of vanilla ice cream. When our cat, Mimi, birthed a litter of kittens in Ben's and my bedroom closet, we asked Mom if we could keep them, and she absently said yes. Soon the kittens contracted some sort of illness, so when you'd pick something off the floor you'd sometimes find a dead kitten underneath. Plus I'd failed to properly crate train OJ, because I had no idea how to do that, and he wouldn't stop relieving himself inside the house.

"Don't let him do that again," growled Dad, angry after stepping in a pile of shit next to his bed.

"But I don't know how to get him to stop," I said.

"You need to shove his nose in his crap, and hold him there," Dad said.

One day, Ben and I were lying on the couch watching TV when Dad walked through the front door. He took a sweeping look around the slovenly living room. His brow furrowed and his head started to shake. It was like watching a kettle boil. My body tightened in anticipation.

"Banzai!" he suddenly screamed, the bizarre cry he used when the house had gotten too disgusting for even him to tolerate. Ben and I leapt to our feet like we'd been shocked with electricity, and began furiously cleaning. I felt the way a fish must feel, one moment swimming serenely, the next yanked into the air by a hook through its face. Dad stood there, fuming. I made sure to stay out of his reach.

I was relieved when he went into the bathroom, leaving the door to the hall open behind him. I could hear the splash of his stream. The toilet flushed and the door to his bedroom opened.

"GODDAMN IT!" he screamed.

When Dad kicked him in the ribs, OJ yelped, that sound that seems to come from the very soul of a dog. I broke for the bedroom.

"Dad, don't hurt him!" I yelled.

I rushed toward the room and just as I got there OJ exploded out of it and past me. I stood there facing my father.

"Clean up the goddamned shit, Sam," he snarled.

He towered above me, rage rippling off him like heat off sunbaked asphalt. My hands were shaking.

"You don't have to hurt him like that, Dad," I said.

"Next time it'll be you," he said. I knew he meant it.

I turned heel and ran for the paper towels. I mopped up the soupy puddle, averting my face. Tears streamed down my cheeks.

I found OJ in the backyard.

"It's okay, boy," I said, petting him until my heart stopped pounding.

A few days later, when I got home from school, I saw the single turd sitting innocently in the center of the living room carpet, as if OJ had left me a present.

"Goddamn it!" I yelled.

I rushed to the backyard in a fury and found OJ lying in the sun. He shrunk back from me. I grabbed his collar and yanked him toward the house, pulling him by the neck.

"Bad dog!" I shouted.

I stood over the shit. OJ was scrambling backwards. It felt like his collar might come off over his head, so I grabbed the folds of skin around his neck. I felt my fingernails dig into his flesh. I pushed his nose into the mess. His scrambling took on a new level of intensity. I could hear his nails scratching at the carpet.

"Bad dog!" I yelled.

He struggled, snorting and whining, but I held strong. I kept jamming his face into the mess, as if to say *look what you did*. Then I let him go. He rushed outside. I went to get paper towels and Formula 409. As I wiped up the mess, my anger cooled. I finished, then walked into the backyard and gathered OJ into my arms.

"Good dog," I said, pressing my face into his fur. "That's a good dog."

A few weeks later, Dad herded Mom, Ben, and me into the gray Cadillac, leaving Daniel behind with a babysitter. At the last moment he called out to OJ to come along, and reached to pet him in the backseat. Mom sat in the front, and I sat in the back with Ben and OJ. We headed to Chinatown for dim sum, a weekend tradition.

We left OJ in the car. We sat around a circular table and I poured tons of sugar into my tea, stirring it with a spoon. Dad knew I was mad at him about our fight the night before—he'd spanked me after OJ shit next to his bed—so he kept looking at me with a silly grin on his face and doing this little dance with his head and shoulders to make me laugh. I fought to maintain an angry visage, but I loved having his full attention, and I couldn't help but smile. Soon Dad started calling out the funny names he'd invented for the Chinese dishes. "We'll have an order of fried paper towels," he said, and Ben and I wriggled and giggled as if we were being tickled. When the food came, we ate fast and hard, and soon we were piling back into the car.

My stomach was bursting and I had to pee, but otherwise I was happy. I stared out the window watching the freeway signs thump by. OJ was over by Ben. Dad was singing to the radio, and everyone was laughing. When we pulled up to the house, I bolted inside so I wouldn't have to wait for the bathroom.

A few hours later, Dad stood up from his chair and said he was going into the office.

"Oh come on, Tony. It's a Sunday," said Mom.

"Do you think money just makes itself?" Dad said, his voice flinty.

I looked up from the Hardy Boys book I was reading, and watched as Dad laced his shoes. I remember thinking it was really quiet. As Dad stood up, slid his jangly keys into his pocket, and started walking toward the door, I remember thinking that something was wrong, and when Dad opened the door, I knew what it was. OJ didn't let the door open without standing sentinel, his tail wagging.

I sat on the couch and waited. When I heard Dad's shout, I wasn't surprised. I got to my feet and walked to the door, slowly, as if I were moving underwater.

As I walked down the path to the driveway, Dad rushed by me. Without looking at me he growled, "Your dog is dead." I heard him yell something at Mom, and I heard her shriek.

The Cadillac was parked at the curb. The back left door stood open. I continued toward it, knowing what I would find but at the same time not able to comprehend. When I neared the car, I felt the heat coming off it. I reached the open door and looked inside.

OJ's body was situated perfectly in the footwell. He fit exactly, as if in a carrying case. He looked peaceful, like he was asleep. Around him, the car was ripped to shreds. The backseats were eviscerated, and yellow Styrofoam stuffing spilled out everywhere. The front seat was worse; maybe it had started there. The dashboard had rips across it, jagged nail tears. The cushions on the inside of the door had been ripped off. The fury of life fighting for its own existence. Urine splattered the front passenger seat.

I took a step closer and gingerly touched OJ on the left hip. It was stiff. I turned and ran.

I burst through the front door and into my parents' room. The air seemed peaceful. Sunlight filtered through the shades. I sat on the edge of their bed. I looked at my lap.

OJ had been left behind in the car. I had left OJ behind in the car. The door was unlocked, but that didn't help him. The Southern California sun had heated it like an oven. I started to imagine what the last five minutes of his life must have looked like, but I couldn't, and I shook my head as if to rid it of those thoughts. My stomach clenched, and I could barely breathe.

My mom came in and sat next to me. I started crying. She put her hand on my back. Then my dad came in and sat on the other side. I looked up at him. He looked angry. I knew that I had done this, but that he had done this, too. I knew that somehow he was the source of my pain, but he was also the only one who could comfort me. He was the most powerful thing I'd ever known. I knew that though I hated him right now, I would soon forgive him and work again to please him. With the resignation of a lifer, I leaned on the man I loved and despised, and wept on his shoulder.

He never had the interior of the car repaired. "Too expensive," he said.

CHAPTER 2

The Cheerleader

◻

I n seventh grade, Ben and I made the finals for History Day
LA, a citywide competition where small groups of students
create six-foot-tall exhibits on historical subjects, and our failure to medal was both a source of intense pain and driving
motivation for the next year, when our project landed us on
Oprah. That year Ben was named a starter for the Academic
Decathlon team; I was selected as an alternate. In short, we
were nerds.

Whereas academics came easy, socializing was hard. It was
tough to make friends but easy to make enemies. Mostly, Ben
and I hung together. We never told Dad how hard things
were at school. For our twelfth birthday, Dad got Ben and
me our own phone line. "Soon you'll be in high school and
the phone will be ringing off the hook," he said. I hoisted a
smile across my face as my stomach sank, knowing that phone
would rarely ring.

Our elementary school, in North Glendale, had been
mostly white and Korean kids, but Woodrow Wilson Middle School in South Glendale was mostly Armenian and His-
panic, with gangs. On the way to class I'd walk by benches full
of silent gang members wearing blank faded sweatshirts and
old Dickies, their eyes matching anyone who passed, lingering

until the opposing gaze was dropped. Sometimes there would be fights; Ben and I would run over to watch.

The other group I noticed was the popular kids, known as the Socs (pronounced so-shiz, short for Socials). They were minicelebrities. During breaks they'd congregate in the middle of the quad, and it was as if they were on stage. Eyes fastened on their perfect teeth and gorgeous hair as they talked and laughed, seemingly unaware of their privileged role. Sometimes the cheerleaders would perform routines at lunch, and when they were finished jumping, clapping, and thrusting their right arms straight into the air, they would make their way over to their fellow Socs.

Girls had recently emerged on my radar. Ben and I would sit at the tables to the side of the quad, shoveling ten-cent chocolate-chip cookies and twenty-five-cent slabs of chocolate cake into our mouths, watching the cheerleaders.

I fantasized about belonging to that group. But I never thought that was really possible, until I met Chrissy Hayes.

Of course, I knew who she was already, but I had never talked to her, never even thought of talking to her. But by the miracle of coincidence, or the loving guidance of a higher power, I was assigned to sit next to her in seventh-grade home ec class, and we became partners.

Chrissy Hayes was a cheerleader. A beautiful, bouncy cheerleader. She wore white Keds with white socks and her yellow, blue, and white cheerleader outfit. When she wasn't dressed as a cheerleader, she wore tight jeans and a tight tee shirt. Her smooth, dark Filipino skin would lighten around her eyes when she smiled. Her long brown hair nestled around her shoulders and sometimes, sitting next to her, I could smell it.

I treated Chrissy as I would have the Queen of England. I stared straight ahead, conscious of my hands and arms and thinking how awkward they were. Before she'd even noticed her pencil had fallen to the floor, I'd have retrieved it and would be delicately restoring it to its proper position. From the corner of my eye I watched her doodling on the margins of her notebook. She always drew dolphins, hundreds of little dolphins.

I was nervous and stiff in her presence, but soon the home ec curriculum took over. We baked cake. I measured; she mixed. She tidied up while I wrote up the results. Chrissy seemed unaware of the social gulf that separated us. Soon she was punching me in the shoulder and making laughing eyes at me when the teacher would admonish students for not acting with "appropriate domestic behavior."

My life *happened* in that class. Lying in bed I'd stare at the ceiling, hands behind my head, reviewing all fifty minutes. I'd envision her giggling, or the brown skin peeking out from between her sweater and skirt.

Of course, there were benefits to me. Other cheerleaders sometimes peeked their heads into class, and if the teacher was on the other side of the room, they'd sneak in to chat with Chrissy. "This brown lump is supposed to be a pineapple upside-down cake," Chrissy said. "But Sam and I destroyed it." The other cheerleaders peeked around Chrissy and smiled at me. Then they returned to their conversation while I scribbled on the hand-in. But I was no longer invisible.

I'd time my exit from class to coincide with Chrissy's departure, stopping midway through packing up to rummage through my backpack. I'd fall into step with her. We'd walk together. Those were my proudest moments.

Chrissy had lots of friends. I noticed her saying hi to some of the tougher-looking guys, the Mexicans. They would stare at me with cool, appraising eyes. Sometimes I saw her over with them during break. Mostly she stood in the center of the quad, talking with the other Socs.

It's funny, the things you remember. I can't tell you the name of a single teacher from junior high. I can't remember a single essay I wrote for class. But I can rattle off the names of the six seventh-grade cheerleaders like I can rattle off my social security number.

One day in home ec, while Chrissy and I were making pound cake ("A pound of butter, pound of milk, pound of flour, and a pound of eggs—that's how it got its name!" whooped the teacher), Chrissy told me her birthday was in two weeks.

"Really?" I replied, immediately blushing at the inanity of my response.

"Yep, really," she said, then broke into a smile and laughed. "Seriously," she pursued, holding back a giggle. I laughed and blushed.

"Like, what day, what date?" I said, the gears in my mind starting to turn.

At home I secreted myself in my room and tore through the pages of catalogues, looking for Chrissy's birthday present. I needed a game changer.

As soon as I flipped the page, I knew I'd found it. Right there in front of me was a little, black tee shirt with three glitter dolphins exploding from the glitter ocean behind them. It was the thoughtfulness of the present that made it perfect. We'd never talked about her dolphins. I asked Mom to help me order it.

Later, Dad asked what we had been doing.

"I'm dating a cheerleader," I replied.

"How are the tits?" he asked.

A few days later, the package arrived. The tee shirt looked small, and less shiny than in the catalogue, but great nonetheless. While I wrapped it, I imagined Chrissy opening it, smiling, and clutching it to her chest. Seeing me in class the next day, she'd give me a peck on the cheek and a squeeze of the hand to let me know that she, too, had feelings. I asked Mom to drive me by her house. I was too bashful to go to the door, so Mom left it on the doorstep.

The next day at lunch, Ben and I ate our cookies and

watched the Socs. Chrissy seemed bouncier than usual, and I was optimistic as I walked toward the home ec classroom. As I breached the doorway, two things happened simultaneously: one, I caught Chrissy Hayes's eye, and two, a thick, muscular hand grabbed my throat and squeezed, pushing me against the doorjamb. I struggled to free the hand from my throat while I attempted to twist my head to see who was choking me, both to no avail. He was stronger than me in the way ninth-grade boys are stronger than seventh-grade boys. His fingers seemed to gain strength as I struggled, tightening in a vise. My eyes whirled back, searching for Chrissy, as terror exploded inside me. *I hope she's not watching*, I thought, a split second before my eyes locked with hers.

When her expression didn't change, I knew that this was because of the shirt.

"Stay the fuck away from Chrissy, you fucking *puto*," he hissed in my ear. Then he laughed—a twisting, vicious laugh—and I realized how gravely I'd miscalculated.

"Little fucking bitch," he spat, and dropped me.

His name was Carlos Rodriguez, Chrissy's ninth-grade boyfriend, I learned later. A gangbanger.

I squatted against the wall, clutching my throat. I tried to act nonchalant, as if I hadn't just been choked out in front of the whole class, in front of Chrissy Hayes. I felt a roaring torrent of shame. *Don't show weakness*, I thought to myself, as the whole world looked at it. After a moment, I stood up and walked into the silent class, jaw clenched and face burning. I walked to my table and saw that Chrissy had switched with one of the other girls from the class, and I sat down and stared straight ahead, trying desperately to hold in the tears that were soaking the backs of my eyes.

CHAPTER 3

Camp Fox

☐

Ben and I were always together, but we weren't exactly friends. He seemed more of an appendage than a separate person. There were benefits to having a constant companion—we'd forever excel at two-man games like Ping-Pong and racquetball. There were also downsides. I never had my own birthday party. We shared a bedroom.

But I didn't mind, because I loved being a twin. I once made Ben memorize a series of numbers, so that when people asked us if we could read each other's mind, I'd whisper a number into their ears, and then close my eyes as if to transmit the number to Ben. When he called out, "Fifty-seven," people would freak out.

But Ben didn't like being a twin. When people asked us who was born first, I'd see Ben grimace as I answered, "Me, by four minutes."

There was one part of being a twin that I didn't like. Ben was smarter than me. Theoretically we had the same DNA, but on every standardized test we ever took, Ben scored higher. Not by a lot—I'd be in the ninety-seventh percentile, Ben the ninety-ninth—but enough to hurt.

By the end of seventh grade, Ben and I had crossed the line from chubby to fat, and we got picked on. A lot. When someone would get in my face or shove me in the school halls, I always backed down, too scared to fight back. Afterward, I'd berate myself for being a coward.

School became something to survive. I couldn't wait for summer, especially the weeklong sleepaway camp Ben and I had signed up for, where we wouldn't know anyone. Maybe things would be different.

In June, Ben and I walked across the gangplank onto the ferry that would transport hundreds of campers to Camp Fox on Catalina Island.

"Where do you want to stand?" I asked Ben.

He looked around and then pointed across the room, to an empty space near a window. Ben and I stood next to each other, looking around the boat. Groups were already forming, threes and fours, newfound friends. I didn't understand how people made friends so easily. I didn't want people to see that I was lonely, so I stuck close to Ben. But inside, I knew that being with Ben was a twin's version of being alone. For shy, insecure boys, it was easier to retreat into the safety of twinness rather than to risk new conversations, new relationships.

The boat rumbled as we pulled away from the dock. As I looked around the room, I hardened my stare. If I wasn't going to make friends, then at least I could look intimidating so no one would fuck with me. A few times I caught someone's eye, but they quickly dropped their gaze.

Then, I caught an eye that didn't drop. It belonged to a large kid with a faded, oversized sweatshirt with "Jorge" on the front. We stared at each other for two seconds until I dropped my eyes. My face grew hot. I sensed him moving toward me. Then he was upon me.

"What the fuck are you looking at?" he said.

His three friends formed a half circle around Ben and me. Ben stood slightly behind me. They looked older. Two of them had chains running from their back pockets to their belts.

I'd never met Jorge, but I knew him. Guys like him were always in my face. I'd made my first enemy in less than fifteen minutes.

"I wasn't looking at anything," I said. I squirmed under his gaze. He moved up on me real tight, his chest almost touching my burning forehead.

"Do something, man. Do something, pussy. What now?"

I just stood there, my heart pounding, paralyzed. I hated him, but I hated myself more. *Coward.* Just then, a counselor started toward us. Jorge saw him and stepped back.

"Watch your back," he said, as he moved away, his friends in tow.

Our cabin was little more than a hut: thatched roof, no walls, and six bunk beds. By the time Ben and I got there, all the lower bunks were taken. I threw my sack on one of the remaining top bunks.

"Hey, what the fuck?" I heard, as a hand jammed my shin, nearly knocking me down.

My muddy shoe was planted on the sleeping bag of the camper below me. "Sorry," I muttered. "But don't push me."

"Don't put your foot on my sleeping bag, then."

I didn't say anything. I heard the other kids laugh.

Our counselor, Okie, gathered everyone outside and explained the schedule: breakfast at seven, then assigned cabin activity, lunch at noon, then free time till dinner, and then a campfire after.

That night we marched single file up the dirt road toward the campfire, until the line halted halfway up. Ben and I stood apart, already on the outs with our cabin mates. I looked down the hill and saw Jorge and his friends about fifty people behind us. I was relieved we wouldn't be sitting close to him.

As if he felt my gaze, he whirled and looked right at me. *Fuck*.

The line started forward. As I crested the hill I saw the blazing, crackling fire in the middle of a semicircle of stadium-style benches. The counselors were jamming the campers in like sardines. I watched the rows fill, coiling like a snake. I realized with horror that Jorge might end up behind me.

Ben and I were pushed into the far side of row four. I started frantically counting how many students there were per row, but lost count and had to start over. Our row filled, and the line snaked back, one level up. Jorge entered the row, and I prayed and prayed that some distance would separate us. *What are the chances?* I protested feebly as Jorge plopped down almost directly behind Ben. Jorge and his friends started as soon as they sat down.

"Bitch," said Jorge.

"Pussy fat twins," one of his friends said.

"What the fuck you looking at?" said another.

I wanted to disappear. I looked over to see if I could engage Okie's attention, but he was deep in conversation with a female counselor. I looked around desperately for someone to help. There was no one. Ben was getting it worse—he was closer—and I was glad for that.

"Fat twins. Fucking fat twins," Jorge said.

Ben and I just stared straight ahead, not even willing to acknowledge our terror to each other. At times like this I hated Ben; our twinness seemed to make us conspicuous targets. I'd be paralyzed with fear, and tortured afterward by impotent rage, and Ben would see all of it.

The camp director walked onstage. I felt a wave of anger gathering behind me. The crowd had just started to quiet when Jorge leaned forward and slugged Ben across the cheek.

Everyone around us froze. I looked over at Ben, whose

hand had gone to his face. He was looking up at Jorge, who towered above him. Ben stared at him for a second, and I thought he might do something. But then he turned away, faced forward. Only I could see his eyes fill with tears.

"You okay?" I whispered.

"No," he said, keeping his brimming eyes forward. I wanted to apologize for getting us into this, but I didn't. After the campfire, Ben and I walked silently back to our cabin and climbed into our bunks without a word.

Jorge and his friends haunted us the entire week. The activity in the morning with our cabin was safe; Jorge was with his own cabin. But afternoons were different. During the three hours of free time, Ben and I existed on the periphery, always on guard against Jorge and his friends, always moving. It seemed everyone was playing and laughing but us. Sometimes we'd make our way to the beach and bodysurf. There was one fat kid who bodysurfed near us, but we kept our distance from him, conspicuous enough.

Late in the afternoons we'd sit wrapped cold and damp in our towels and watch the campers waiting in line for tubing. Each cabin had been assigned one time slot for tubing, and ours was the last day. A large, inflatable tube roped to the back of a speedboat would drag the campers, one by one, into the ocean.

By the last day of camp, Ben and I were refugees, stumbling around, seeking asylum. We were sunburned, exhausted, and friendless. It was our turn for tubing, and Ben and I were near the front of the line.

"I'm a little nervous," I said to Ben, and he nodded. The kid ahead of me squealed as he was dragged toward open water. I was next. The counselor looked down at me.

"Thumbs-up means you want to go faster," he said. "Thumbs-down means slow it down. If you fall off, just stay where you are and let the boat circle around for you. Hold on tight to the handles or they'll slip. And have fun. Remember to have fun."

The boat dragged the tube into my reach. I held the dock with my right hand as I leaned out with my left to grasp the handle tightly. Straining, I lowered my body facedown onto the tube, which skimmed across the water.

The man in the boat smiled at me and gave a thumbs-up. I took a deep breath and gave one back. The boat pulled away. The line snapped taut. It felt like my arms might rip from their sockets. I suddenly understood how powerful the engine was, and I was scared.

The water sprayed up and knifed my face. I couldn't open my eyes. The tube bounced higher and higher. I wasn't giving a thumbs-up or a thumbs-down—I was holding on for dear life. My forearms were straining and my fingers started to slip but a rush of adrenaline allowed me to close my grip.

Suddenly, the collisions got harder and the bounces higher and I knew we had reached open water. Whap, whap, WHAP, the ocean slammed the tube. WHAP, WHAP, WHAP. The water felt solid, like concrete. I gasped for breath as the air crushed my lungs. I moaned through clenched teeth.

Then it happened.

I saw the boat turn; we had gone as far out as we were going to go—to the middle of the ocean—and we were turning back. The turning boat made a huge wake, frothy and raging. The rope to the boat strained from the centrifugal force. I was on a collision course with that wake. I was going to hit it dead-on.

The tube hit the wake like a freight train. My feet flew into the air as I held my desperate grip on the handles. For a moment I enjoyed a reprieve from the battering waves. Then, I felt the tube start to turn. *No, please God no*. As I sailed through the air, clutching my lifeline, I saw the tube move out from below me, turning on its side. The water opened up beneath me.

With a great smack, I slammed into the ocean. The tube flipped upside down. I couldn't breathe, but still I clung to the handles. I knew I had to let go, but I was afraid. Finally my fingers loosened, and I felt the tube rip away. Then I was somersaulting underwater.

I didn't know which way was up. I jerked around, caught in my now-loosened life jacket, choking and desperate for air. I opened my mouth but instead of air I inhaled a wave. Salt-water stung my throat. I choked and gagged. My life jacket bunched up by my ears, trapping my arms, obscuring my view. It felt like I might slip out of it.

I was able to take in only a quick breath before I was hammered again by another wave. When I finally surfaced, I began to cry.

The sea seemed to calm. I looked around. The boat was nowhere to be seen. For miles, all I could see was black ocean. No land. No boats. No humans.

Each time I kicked I was afraid my leg might rub against a shark, common in those waters. The weight of my body seemed too heavy for the flimsy life jacket. The water was rising above my jawline. The feel of water entering my ears drove me to a frenzy, and I kicked furiously until I tired and sank once more. I cried and flailed. I thought I was going to die.

I was dizzy from the cold and lack of air. My breathing was jagged, gasping. The terror of the moment, the fear and humiliation from the week, from my whole life, rushed over me. My neck slipped under the water, then my mouth, then the top of my head. I was completely submerged, in the middle of the ocean.

Then something happened. Terror and humiliation collided, and it was as if an atom had been split. Where there had been fear a moment before, now there was fury. With deep, heaving strokes I willed myself out of the water, chest high. No longer was I slipping underneath; my legs churned determinedly beneath me. I would swim back if I had to, goddamn it.

At the top of a swell, I caught sight of the boat in the distance, heading toward me. I was ready to tear apart anyone that came at me. The boat drew past me, and I glared at the driver. He was laughing. The tube arrived, and with a kick I propelled myself up on it. My fingers slipped as I tried to grasp the handles, and again I sank below the surface. Three times I tried, and three times I slipped, falling into the icy water. The fourth time, I closed my grip on the handles and held on for my life.

I signaled a thumbs-down.

When I got back to the pier, I slid from the tube and frantically dog-paddled to the ladder. The driver called after me, but I ignored him. As I pulled myself up, my limbs started shaking.

"Are you okay?" Ben asked. "What happened?"

"I fell off," I said.

"I'm sorry," he said. "Do you want me to stay?"

I told him no, and sat on the beach, numb from the cold and the fear. As I waited for Ben, I thought about what had happened out there. Something had changed inside me.

When Ben returned, we walked back in silence to the cabin. It was the last day of camp, and we had an hour to pack up our belongings. I toweled off and put on damp and dirty clothes. Ben kept looking up at me, but I didn't speak. It seemed impossible to explain. I felt hardened, seared.

Just as I was finishing packing, I saw movement from the corner of my eye and looked up to see Jorge and his three friends approaching our cabin.

It wasn't that I didn't feel fear—I was as scared as I always had been. It just didn't matter as much anymore. *Fuck it.*

"Come on, you fucking pussy twins. Let's go. Get the fuck out here."

I saw the surprise on his face as I strode toward him.

"Fuck you," I said.

His friends cheered but his face dropped. My face felt slack. He started to run toward me. He took two steps and then leapt into the air, a jump kick. I caught him in midair, rolled my hips, and threw him into the corner post of the cabin, moving after him. He hit it with a crunch, fell to the grass, and I was on him. In a panic-driven rage, I attacked him with fists, forearms, and knees. I never felt my hands hit him, but I saw red marks on his face and rips in his shirt.

A counselor pulled me off. I could see Jorge's eyes. They were afraid. I was thrilled. The counselor pushed me back. Jorge remained on the ground. I ripped myself from the counselor's arms and turned and walked away. I heard Ben following behind me.

When we got to the rocks on the beach where no one could see us, we sat in silence.

Then the feelings came. Whooping gasps. Stomach-heaving sobs. Tears poured from my eyes and I leaned against Ben, shuddering. After a time, the convulsions slowed, then passed. My heartbeat leveled. I felt calm, but raw.

"Oh my God," Ben said. "You fucked him up. I can't believe it."

I didn't say anything, but my chest swelled a bit with pride. We stared out at the ocean for a few seconds.

"What happened?" Ben asked. I knew there was no way he could understand what had happened to me out there in the water. I tried to explain anyway.

"I felt like I was going to disappear," I said. "Like I was nothing. I *won't* feel like that anymore. I don't care who it is, how tough they are. I'm not backing down."

I could see he didn't understand. How could I explain that

I had become someone else? Someone bigger. How could I explain how powerful I felt, and how excited that made me? But also sad, for the loss of that little boy I'd once been, who'd silently slipped out of the life jacket and sank down into the ocean, until he'd disappeared so completely that it was as if he'd never existed at all.

CHAPTER 4

Numbcake

◻

A year later, my family pulled up to Indra, a Thai restaurant in Glendale that we frequented three or four times a month. There were four kids now—Ben and I were thirteen, Daniel was six, and Julia was five—and we were regulars. When the pretty Thai woman at the front saw us, she directed us to our usual table.

Dad motioned for the waitress and began rattling off the standard order: pad Thai, barbecue chicken, spicy green beans with chicken, eggplant with pork, Indian-noodle soup, and seafood curry.

"Tony, I want the spicy fish," said Mom.

The table went quiet. Mom sat with her shoulders hunched, her large body angled to the side, as if to deflect a blow. She hated how Dad ordered without asking what anyone wanted. She was jealous of his sway over us, how he could overrule her just by speaking, how we begged him to take us on "special time."

I felt a burst of anger. Why did she start up like this? I liked the spicy fish, too, but it was *too expensive*. Even then, I'd begun to wish I had a different mom. Not just for me but for Dad.

When Dad and I were on special time, we'd go to a hole-in-the-wall Korean place or a Mexican place in East LA. He'd have a couple drinks. In the car on the way home, Dad would talk about how unhappy he was in his marriage. If it weren't for the kids, he said, he'd have left long ago. He stayed for us.

I'd nod somberly, while inside I was overjoyed that Dad respected me enough to share his deepest feelings. I never loved him more than in those moments. "I really respect what you've done as a father," I'd say. He'd nod, tears in his eyes. Then we'd go into the house, both furious at Mom.

Dad glared at Mom. To people who didn't know our family, asking for spicy fish might seem like a regular request, but I saw that it was a direct attack from the woman who'd forced him to work, let herself get fat, and trapped him in a loveless marriage. His eyes narrowed; he ordered the spicy fish.

I leapt into the silence that followed. "How's work?" I said to Dad.

"Shitty," Dad said. "I didn't get the account. Close as a cunt hair."

I giggled.

"Tony!" Mom said.

"Oh fuck off, Linda," he said, and we kids stared at the table.

"Work is going good for me," I offered, hoping to re-establish the peace. Ben and I were selling newspapers door-to-door. A couple times a week, a pickup truck rolled by our house and we jumped in the back with a few other kids. The boss drove to a new neighborhood and dropped each of us off on a different street to knock on doors.

"I was the top seller again this week," I continued.

Dad smiled. "Oh yeah?" He turned to Ben. "What about you?"

Ben's face reddened.

Just then the food arrived, and relief flashed across Ben's face; he didn't have to answer. Hands reached out before the plates even hit the table. After everyone's plates were filled, silence descended around the table. This was the part I loved. The tension between my parents, the sarcasm and teasing, all faded into a Christmas Eve cease-fire so we could eat our spicy green beans with chicken. The only sounds were forks on plates and heavy breathing. After the last bowl was emptied, the last plate scraped, we sank down in our seats with loud groans. Heads at other tables turned to look at us. The waitress cleared the dishes. What remained on the table was disgusting. Rice everywhere, splashes of sauce, noodles strewn about—it looked like we'd eaten without plates. But there was no electricity in the air, no wisecracks, no tension.

"I need to get out," said Julia. "I have to go to the bathroom."

"Go ahead," Dad said, not moving. Dad was on the end. He needed to stand up for her to slide out of the booth.

"Dad!" she whined.

"You know the rules, Julia," he said. Once he'd sat down, he wouldn't get up.

"Fine," she said, infuriated. She slithered down under the table and began crawling through the jungle of hairy legs.

By the time Julia returned, the single dessert Dad had ordered, a sweet bean pie called Mah-Gang, was gone. As we stood to leave, Julia began to whine.

"I didn't get *anything* for dessert," she said. "It's not *fair*."

Outside, Julia stood at the window of the Circle K convenience store next door, pleading for Dad or Mom to buy her a Suzy Q. Mom fished a couple dollars from her purse and handed them to Julia.

We squeezed into Dad's gray Cadillac, the four children in the back, the interior still carrying the scars from OJ's death. Julia sat on Ben's lap. She hunched her body around the Suzy Q as she opened it, but she didn't have a chance. First, Ben reached around her from the left and swiped his finger through the thick cream in the middle of the cake sandwich. She whirled, yelling "Stop!" As she did, I reached from her blind side and pulled off a chunk. She whirled back, infuriated. Daniel reached over and grabbed a handful of her treat and stuffed it into his mouth, laughing. "Stop! Stop! It's *mine*!" Julia screamed, as tears poured down her cheeks.

"Shut the fuck up back there," Dad yelled.

The next night, Dad took Daniel, Ben, and me to Fender Benders, a fifties diner known for its signature dessert—the Bender, a plate piled high with chocolate-frosted chocolate cake, vanilla ice cream, whipped cream, chocolate sauce, nuts, and a cherry. Every time Dad brought us here, we begged for the Bender. He almost never relented. But on that night, he ordered it. He'd gotten furious at how we'd fought with each other over dessert the night before. He wanted to teach us how to eat "like civilized people."

Dad sat at the head of the table, the untouched Bender already melting before him. All eyes were glued to the dessert. "We are going to eat like people, tonight. Slowly. In control. One by one."

He dug his spoon into the very top of the Bender, taking the cherry, much of the chocolate sauce, and a large portion of the whipped cream. We watched as he chewed slowly, staring at each of us in turn. He waited until his mouth was completely empty before he pushed the plate to his left, toward Ben.

That he chose Ben devastated me. I watched helplessly as Ben scooped an enormous bite of cake, ice cream, and the rest of the whipped cream, my favorite.

"Smaller," Dad barked. "Put it back. Greedy fuck."

Ben looked embarrassed, angry. "You said one bite. It's one bite."

"I said put it back," Dad said. For a moment Ben's eyes hardened in defiant scorn, but Dad stared him down. Ben dumped his bite back. He scooped a smaller one and ate it

34

without looking up. When he was done, he shoved the plate toward Daniel.

By the time it reached me, the whipped cream was gone. I took as big a bite as I thought I could get away with, and then passed it to Dad. Each time someone took a bite, I'd either celebrate or grieve, depending on the toppings they consumed.

The dessert was nearly gone when it once again reached Dad. He took an enormous bite. I heard Ben exhale in frustration. No one said anything. Dad passed the plate to Ben. One bite remained. Ben looked at Daniel's near-panicked face. Then he pushed the plate toward Daniel, who finished it off. As we walked to the car, my eyes filled with tears. It wasn't fair. Everyone else had gotten more than me.

A few weeks later I found myself home alone for the afternoon. I took all the cushions off the couches, reached deep into the crevices until I'd found every quarter, dime, and nickel that had fallen there. Soon I'd collected seven dollars.

I biked to the corner store and purchased a half gallon of chocolate-chip ice cream, whipped cream, and all the ingredients for a Betty Crocker chocolate cake mix. I baked the cake and when it cooled, I smeared the whole thing with chocolate frosting. I piled on mounds and mounds of chocolate-chip ice cream. I shook the can of whipped cream and sprayed until every bit was covered, as if by snow. Then I sat down at the table and ate, and ate, and ate. When I felt sick, I rested, then ate some more. When I finished, I stood up woozily and walked toward the couch. But I didn't make it—I veered off to the bathroom, knelt before the toilet, and vomited everything up.

CHAPTER 5

Chicken-All-Together

▢

When Dad moved the family to a rented house in La Cañada—an effete suburb on the outskirts of LA—so Ben and I could attend the excellent public high school, I saw an opportunity for reinvention. I got my ear pierced and bought baggy jeans and a chain wallet.

La Cañada High School was small—three hundred students per grade—so our arrival set off a ripple of excitement. That first week, I received intricately folded handwritten notes from Stephanie Dodge and a girl named Mouse. I was attracted to both of them, especially Mouse. But as the week wore on, I realized Mouse and Stephanie were not part of the incrowd, so I ignored them. I wanted the popular girls.

I was fourteen and feverish with hormones. After school I'd sneak into my parents' room and pluck out the *Penthouse Forum*s my dad kept in his bedside table. In the sanctuary of my own room—for the first time, Ben and I didn't have to share—I'd read the erotic stories and masturbate over and over until I was exhausted.

I figured since there were no gangs at La Cañada, I could be the tough guy. Those first few weeks, I stared down several guys in the hallway and was thrilled when they dropped their eyes. One day I stared down a short guy whose muscles bulged underneath his sweatshirt. He dropped his eyes, but with a smirk on his lips. That afternoon six guys surrounded me at my locker. The short muscular guy stepped forward. I thought he was going to say something, but then my right ear exploded, and my vision went black. When I came to, I was crumpled on the ground. The hallway was empty. I stayed home for a week, too humiliated to return to school.

A few months into freshman year, Ben started dating a girl named Emma Ramsdale. She had pimples, braces, no curves. But Ben liked her, and soon she was his girlfriend.

It was the first time either of us had a girlfriend, and I was jealous. I was also surprised. Since elementary school, things had been easier for me socially than for Ben. We were both nerds, but Ben took more flak than I did. He was always the smartest kid in school and, like many geniuses, had rough, abrasive edges. His sarcastic lash of a tongue, sweatpants, and thick glasses made him a frequent target. Toward the end of junior high, he'd started spending lunch alone in the library, studying algebra, because in the school yard he'd get picked on. And he was too scared to fight back.

But in high school he found refuge in Emma. She adored him. She was always over at our house. I became friends with her. Sometimes when she called for Ben, I'd talk to her on the phone for a few minutes before putting Ben on. I liked talking to Emma and wanted to be included.

That feeling only intensified when I was first invited over to Emma's house, with Ben. Her house was everything ours was not. It was immaculate. The refrigerator was stocked. Emma's mom cooked dinner every night. They ate together as a family.

Our Guatemalan housekeeper would leave a pot of spaghetti or greasy chicken on the kitchen table for dinner. We'd all eat at different times, in front of the TV. On weekends, Dad would order pizza, but in an effort to save money he'd order just one. You had to eat fast to get a second piece. Once I took a piece into the bedroom and hid it in a drawer. Then I went back, got another slice, and ate it slowly, savoring it. Mrs. Ramsdale would make home-cooked meals like Chicken-All-Together, a golden-brown chicken and cheese casserole. There was always enough for seconds.

When her husband walked through the door, they stood in the kitchen kissing and whispering. When my parents were in the same room, it was like being in a tank with two angry whales. I loved that the Ramsdales were still in love, and I harbored an innocent crush on Mrs. Ramsdale.

I wanted to spend as much time as I could at the Ramsdales'. I loved the cleanliness, the order. I loved being in a house where the parents weren't at war. Emma didn't seem to mind, but I could tell Ben didn't want me there. But still I came. As the months passed, Emma herself started to develop. One day I noticed that her stick-figure body all of a sudden had legs, breasts.

For a while, I ignored my attraction and held to the delusion that since Emma and I were friends, I had equal invitation to be at their house. That idea was smashed when Emma's family invited Ben, and not me, along for their annual Lake Tahoe family vacation. I asked Mrs. Ramsdale questions about the trip agenda, to make clear that I was available. But they never invited me. I was at their house as they loaded the van for the drive. I waved as they pulled away.

A few months after the Lake Tahoe trip, I was still hanging around Emma's house, and Ben had finally had enough. We were in the Ramsdales' living room with Emma and her younger brother. Ben and I were arguing. I said what I thought was the winning line and was smiling proudly when Ben retorted, "Why don't you leave? No one wants you around."

A nervous silence descended on the room. Ben and Emma's brother went outside to throw the football. A minute later, we followed them, and when Ben was running backwards, his eyes on a high-thrown ball, I ran up and slugged him on the jaw. Ben was now bigger than me, but I knew he wouldn't do anything. He was still scared to fight. He didn't seem hurt. He just stared at me scornfully, until I turned tail and ran down the street.

At the end of freshman year, my closest friend, Nate Robertson, said, "Wow, you are really getting fat." It was true. I'd weighed myself the day before—210 pounds. At every meal, I ate until I was stuffed, chasing numbness.

I laughed off Nate's comment, keeping a straight face so he wouldn't see how much his words stung. Later that day, for the first time, I decided to go on a diet.

I ate three times per day, about three hundred calories per meal: a small bowl of cereal, a bagel, or a turkey sandwich with no cheese or mayo. I literally counted down the minutes till my next meal. I'd get in bed shortly after dinner in hopes that I could fall asleep before getting hungry, but soon I would be tossing and turning, taking sips of water to cool the burning coals in my stomach.

That summer I lost forty pounds.

Then, at the beginning of sophomore year, Ben went out for the wrestling team. I knew he didn't want me to follow. He had installed a lock on his bedroom door, one of those fragile slide bolts you find on bathroom stalls. I could have knocked it down with one kick, but its symbolism was obvious. He wanted distance from me, but I missed him and looked up to him, so I joined the wrestling team, too.

Wrestling is the perfect sport for a chubby kid dying to be tough. I began that first year wrestling in a 170-pound weight class but soon dropped to 160 pounds to fill an open varsity spot. In the off-season Ben and I went to wrestling camps and drove all over Southern California to compete in freestyle tournaments. By junior year, we were decent.

At practice I was always paired with Ben, which I hated. Whenever I went for his legs, it felt like getting in a car crash. It soon became clear he was the better wrestler.

I was getting tired of losing to Ben. In tenth grade, I scored 1400 on the PSATs. Ben scored 1510. During a bathroom break in the middle of the SATs, the most important test either of us had ever taken, I told Ben I'd missed at least three questions.

"I'm getting a perfect," he said. And he had been right. He was physically larger than me, stronger, and a better wrestler. He had better hair than I did. Even his goals were bigger than mine. At the beginning of junior year he posted a piece of paper above his bedroom door that read:

Ben Polk, Goals
- California State Wrestling Champion
- 1600 SATs
- Bench press 350 pounds
- Run five-minute mile
- Straight As

Every time I saw that sign, I felt diminished. A few months into junior year, Ben and Emma broke up. I gave it about a week and then started showing up at her house. Without Ben there, I felt less obtrusive, and fell into the easy machinations of a family's routine. Now Mrs. Ramsdale would smile at me—just me—as I sat across from her at the dinner table. I would help Emma's brother with his homework. And I would spend time alone with Emma.

At first it was innocent—we'd study or watch TV together. But I still felt guilty. When I'd hear a car pull into the cul-de-sac, I'd rush to the window terrified that I'd see Ben driving up. From Emma's house I took a circuitous path home to obfuscate where I'd been. But nothing had happened.

Then, things started to happen. Small things. I helped Emma stretch, my chest against her back on the floor of her bedroom. We started sunbathing on her porch, and I would accidentally brush my hand across her legs. After a while, I started leaving my hand where it touched her. She didn't object. I think we both enjoyed that we were crossing a line. But the line kept moving. I started stroking her legs, closer and closer to her bikini bottom. But still, I believed, nothing really untoward had happened.

And then, something untoward happened. We didn't sleep together, but for a few glorious nights we did everything else.

After a few hookups, Emma stopped it. Of course, I never told Ben. A couple of months later, Ben and Emma got back together. He started to go again to her house, and sometimes she'd come over to ours. I'd greet her casually, as if nothing had happened.

But something had happened. And though Ben didn't know for sure, he must have sensed something. Ben and I had both started drinking that year, egged on by guys on the wrestling team, who taught us how to casually slide bottles of peach schnapps under our tee shirts and smuggle them from the grocery store. But over the past few months, I'd started to suspect that Ben wasn't just drinking with the wrestlers, but also alone in his room.

One night, I was in my room with Claire, a girl who'd progressed from platonic friend to shameful secret hookup to publicly acknowledged girlfriend. Ben was in his room with Emma. I went to the bathroom, and when I headed back toward my room, I passed Ben in the hall. My shoulder bumped his as we passed.

"What the fuck?" he said.

"What?" I said.

"Fuck you," he said.

"What are you even talking about? Fuck *you*."

He came up on me fast and put his forehead against mine. I saw a rage in his eyes that I'd never seen before.

"Do something," he sneered.

"Fuck off," I said.

He hit me in the face. My head rocked backwards. I didn't so much feel pain as register the massive force of the impact. I stood there in the hallway, with blood running down my chin, and gaped at him.

"Hit me," he said.

"No," I said. He hit me again. His eyes were frantic. I could see he wasn't going to stop. I couldn't lift my arms. Not only was I now terrified of my brother; I was also thick with guilt. I deserved this. He hit me again. I took it. As he hauled back to punch me again in the face, my dad rushed out of his room and threw himself between us. I went into my room, sat on the bed, and burst into tears.

CHAPTER 6

Fifteen Pounds

◻

By senior year in high school, I was no longer fat—veins snaked my forearms and my shoulders. A thick layer of muscle covered my arms and back. My hair was bleached, mimicking how wrestlers from Temecula Valley and Calvary Chapel, two of the toughest programs in the state, wore their hair. The previous summer, Ben and I had gone to several wrestling camps, including a two-week intensive that was billed as the toughest camp in the nation. Every day after school Ben and I drove an hour and a half to East LA to practice with the wrestlers at Schurr High School, a regional powerhouse.

For senior season I cut down to 152 pounds. It was grueling—I was cutting 8 to 9 pounds of water weight for each match—but I loved how small my opponents were, how easy to throw. Midway through the season, I started to consider dropping even lower, to 145 pounds.

To qualify for state at a certain weight class, you had to wrestle several tournaments at that weight. The California Interscholastic Federation was concerned about the health risks of dropping excessive water weight. If I wanted to drop to 145 pounds, the match versus San Marino was my last chance.

The day before the San Marino match, I stood alone in the cold gray locker room on a cold gray scale. I hadn't eaten since the night before. I took a deep breath and started sliding the metal cartridge over the grooves. As I passed 155 my stomach tightened; I thought I'd dropped a few pounds that week. The metal finger didn't drop until I hit 160. *Holy shit*, I thought. *I have to cut 15 pounds in one day.*

I pulled on mesh shorts, a tee shirt, and then two pairs of sweatpants and sweatshirts. *I'm already hot*, I thought plaintively, as I pulled on a pair of plastics over the sweats. Plastics are trash-bag suits with elastic at the wrists, neck, and ankles that cinch, trapping the heat inside. I looked like an astronaut. I put on a ski hat.

I was an hour early to practice, so I jogged around the perimeter of the mat, the squeak of my ASICS my only company. Practice was brutal, two straight hours of intense drilling and hard wrestling. After, I lay exhausted on the mat. I hadn't drunk any water during practice. I figured I had dropped six or seven pounds. My mouth was parched and I fantasized about a sip of water. But I knew this was only the beginning. I got up, walked out into the warm Los Angeles air, and started to run. I followed the trail the cross-country team trained on, each footfall bringing a brown puff of dirt. It was already difficult to swallow.

After three miles I headed back to the locker room. I stripped, toweled off, and stepped on the scale: 153 pounds. Not even halfway. Ben was dropping a weight class, too, and had to cut almost as much as I did. Even though we weren't really speaking, it felt comforting to be with him. We walked to the car in silence, our mouths dry and lips chapped.

At the YMCA, we undressed, wrapped towels around our waists. We each held a credit card as we pulled open the wooden door, revealing the dark maw of the sauna. The air singed my face, and the scalding wood burned the back of my legs. Soon I was sweating. Sweat is a cooling mechanism; as it evaporates from your skin, heat leaves your body.

I started to scrape the sweat off with the credit card. The more I scraped off, the more my body produced, desperately trying to cool itself. First one arm, long swipes from shoulder to wrist, then the other. Then chest, stomach, sides, calves, thighs, face, and neck. Then again, in rhythm. Scrape, scrape, scrape, switch hands, scrape, scrape, scrape. Sweat pooled below me.

I'd committed to ten full credit card circuits of my body. Halfway through, I started to panic. I wanted to run out, drink water, quit wrestling. But I didn't. I wanted to go to state. I wanted to wrestle in college. And I kept thinking about what had happened with my dad the weekend before.

The whole family was at Manhattan Beach, a forty-minute drive from our house. Dad and I started wrestling. I thought we were just fooling around when suddenly my foot slipped in the sand and I went down. He ended up on top of me, his heavy belly covering my face. He let out a triumphant whoop, loud enough so heads snapped toward us. I lay grimacing underneath him, waiting for him to get off. But he didn't get up.

"Big wrestler guy," he taunted, holding me down. "Still can't beat your old man."

"Get off me!" I yelled, arching my back and pushing him off.

He fell back but kept his arms high in the air, triumphant.

"Never going to beat your old man," he said.

But I didn't want to beat him. I just wanted him to be proud of me. That incident stayed with me all week. I'd remember the feeling of Dad on top of me, and my jaw would clench with resentment. In the sauna, I steeled myself for the excruciating pain I knew was still ahead of me. Sweat was still coming off me in buckets—it was when you stopped sweating that things became really hard. I watched proudly as my puddle grew.

My mind was a single camera, orbiting around an ice-cold lemon-lime Gatorade. Droplets of water condensed on the bottle. One slid down like a tear.

Eventually the panic and heat overwhelmed me, and I rushed out and lay on a bench, touching the metal lockers with my hand to feel their coolness. I savored that cool for five minutes and then, head hung like a prisoner, I reentered that dark oven.

After three hours of fifteen minutes in, five minutes out, Ben and I went home to endure a long, sleepless night. In the morning I was still two pounds over. After classes, I grimly piled on my damp layers of sweats and shuffled along the same dusty trail I'd run the day before. The sun beat down, but no sweat came.

Coach was in the locker room when I returned. He was angry that I was still a pound over. He put me in the front seat of his car, rolled up the windows, and turned the heater up full blast. While he drove, I sucked on Jolly Ranchers, spitting the saliva into a plastic cup. Coach's face was dripping, but I didn't start sweating until twenty-five minutes in.

I was still a half pound over when we got back but was too parched to do anything. I stripped to my underwear and lay on the cool stone floor, shifting positions every few minutes to new slabs to conduct away the heat. I kept sucking on the Jolly Ranchers, spitting toward the drain next to my head. My teeth hurt, like the enamel had been ripped off of them.

The San Marino wrestlers arrived. Each team lined up in their underwear according to weight. One by one opponents stepped on the scale, and the ref released the metal finger. If it moved, even by a little, the wrestler made weight. My opponent looked tiny. I couldn't believe I was trying to weigh what he weighed.

When it was my turn, I stepped on the scale. The ref removed his finger. The metal finger didn't move. I was still too heavy.

I pulled off my underwear and stepped bare assed onto the scale. I was dizzy. I watched the metal finger as the referee dropped his hand.

It moved. Just barely, but it moved.

Before I was even conscious of it, I'd drained a Gatorade in one swoop. It wasn't pleasurable or enjoyable; it was simply gone, and I was suddenly freezing. I was gulping water, but I still felt as thirsty as before. Soon I was shivering. I put my sweats back on but was still cold. I started to munch on whole wheat bread, and after a while I was full and I knew I was in trouble. The match was in an hour.

The stands were pretty full for a wrestling match, maybe fifty people. Dad was standing at the side of the mat, talking on his cell phone. He'd recently started a public relations business, Polk Communications, and he worked incessantly. It was just him alone in an office, but he'd started to talk about how one day he'd sell the company for millions of dollars. As we warmed up, liquid sloshed inside my stomach. I kept looking at Dad to see if he was watching me, but he was engrossed in his call. The ref blew the whistle, beginning the 103-pound match. I felt nauseous, already exhausted.

Before I knew it I was up next. I took my warm-ups off and walked slowly to the center of the mat.

My opponent was soft and pudgy, a fish. Novice wrestlers are called fish because of how they flop around when you put them on their backs. I towered over him. The whistle blew and he shot. The shot is the most common offensive move in wrestling, sort of a controlled tackle. I saw it coming and scooted away easily. We circled each other again, and then I shot, got ahold of the back of his legs, and lifted him easily into the air. I carried him on my shoulder while he wriggled like a live tuna. The crowd screamed. I heard my dad cheering. I strutted around the mat, then slammed him down, holding him on his back to earn points. I was up 5-0.

I could have kept him on his back, maybe pinned him right then. But the screams from the crowd filled me with pride; I didn't want it to be over yet. So I let him turn to his stomach. Then I just stood up. Letting someone up in wrestling is like slapping them in the face. You *give* them a point, because you know you can earn it back. He stood up uncertainly, unwilling to believe I had so startlingly disrespected him. I walked back to the center of the mat. He started toward me.

We circled each other, and then I shot again, and again lifted him into the air. I heard Dad yell, "Twice!" and I felt proud. But the fish seemed heavier now, and this time I didn't slam him but just dropped him. I could only keep him on his back for a second. I was up 9-1, and there were just a few seconds left in the first period. I was grateful that the fish didn't struggle much as time ran out.

The next round started with the fish on bottom. I formed a diamond shape with my hands, my palms facing out. That was a signal to the referee that I was intentionally letting the fish stand up, giving him another free point. The referee signaled to the fish that he was being let up, and I saw him stiffen at the blatant disrespect. I put my hands on his back and waited for the ref to blow the whistle. When he did, the fish started to stand up. But I wasn't satisfied with just letting him up. I wanted to embarrass him. As he got to his feet I shoved him. He lost his balance, stumbled forward. The crowd laughed. The score was 9-2. The fish came at me with a frantic energy that I recognized. I knew how it felt to be publicly humiliated.

All of a sudden, my body felt hot, like sunburn. The fish shot and I sprawled away but just barely. Then I tried a shot and this time didn't even touch his legs. There was a lot of time left on the clock, but I was out of gas.

I hoped the fish wouldn't sense how weak I'd become, but he did and came at me. I backed up on my heels and the crowd was silent as he pushed me out of bounds. We returned to the center, the ref blew his whistle, and again the fish pushed me out of bounds, this time making a frustrated gesture to the referee, who hit me with a warning for stalling. The next time would cost me a point. I was grateful when I heard the bell end the second round. I put my hands atop my head and sucked in gulps of air but couldn't catch my breath.

I chose neutral position to start the next round. I felt like I was underwater. He shot and I thought I'd blocked him, but then I felt his hands grab my legs and I was suddenly toppling backwards.

"Two points," yelled the ref, a little too happily.

Now I was on my stomach, the fish on top. The score was 9-4. I tried to get up, and he hit me with a vicious cross-face—almost a punch, but legal as long as he used his forearm. Someone yelled, "Oh, that hurt," and I felt a surge of rage but was too weak to do anything about it. I spread my arms and legs flat so he couldn't turn me to my back. I wasn't even trying to escape. It was blatant stalling. But there was nothing else I could do. He hit me with another vicious cross-face, his forearm against my teeth, and I knew this was purely retributive. Now *he* was playing to the crowd, and if I hadn't been so exhausted I would have been livid, but instead I was terrified. The ref blew the whistle and docked me another stalling point. I was gasping for breath and thought I might faint. Then I had the worst feeling I've ever had. I felt like I was going to shit myself in front of everyone. I desperately tried to maintain control of my sphincter, as I imagined the horrible silence that would come when the crowd saw poop sliding down my leg.

The ref hit me for stalling again, but there were just thirty seconds left, and I knew he wouldn't hit me with four more stall points. I was going to win the match. I was fighting tears on one end, my bowels on the other. I stayed on my stomach while the fish grunted above me, cross-facing at will, my face purple. The bell rang; the match ended.

The crowd was silent as I slowly made my way to my knees, then stood up. I reached across and shook the hand of the sneering fish, and then the ref held my hand in the air. I was supposed to shake hands with the opposing coach, but instead I beelined to the door. Outside, I spied a clump of bushes where I could hide and collapsed into it. I was dry heaving and convulsing, and I felt like my bowels would let go at any second. But they didn't, and I lay there, alone, until Ben came to find me.

"Where's Dad?" I asked.

"He left," Ben said.

Neither Ben nor I made state that year. We both lost in sectionals. On the day of the state tournament, we filled a cooler with beer and drove five hours to watch. We sat in an empty corner of the stands and got drunk, watching the other wrestlers live the fantasy we had chased but failed to realize.

Ever since I'd accompanied Dad on a business trip to New York, I'd dreamed about going to Columbia University. Ben dreamed of Princeton. We both applied for early decision. A coach I had trained with at Schurr High, the tough program in East LA, knew the coach at Columbia, and even though I hadn't placed at state, the Columbia coach added me to the roster without ever seeing me wrestle. I had great SAT scores but hadn't been the kind of straight-A student that usually got into Columbia.

The day I received my fat envelope from Columbia, Ben received a thin one from Princeton. Devastated, he applied to every other Ivy League university. They all rejected him, except for Cornell. Crushed, he accepted.

The next year, three college wrestlers—Billy Saylor (Campbell University), Joseph LaRosa (University of Wisconsin), and Jeff Reese (University of Michigan)—died cutting weight. Reese was cutting the most. He was trying to shed 17 pounds in a day, to make the 150-pound weight class.

CHAPTER 7

There's a Bomb in My Stomach

◻

I arrived in New York on a red-eye flight with a suitcase, a laptop computer, a hundred bucks in my pocket, and a warning from Dad that no more money would be forthcoming. He'd taken out loans to pay for tuition and room and board and said I'd need to find a job to cover living expenses. My room was barren, except for the wall I covered with Absolut Vodka ads.

I was desperate to carve out a place for myself at Columbia, to belong. In high school, the noon bell would ring and I'd join the stream of students headed to the parking lot, keeping a hopeful eye out as students merged into groups of threes and fours and drove to a fast-food lunch. Sometimes, I'd catch an invite, but usually the crowd would thin, and at the last possible moment I'd turn purposefully off toward the locker rooms. I'd circle back and head toward the empty halls of the school building where I would find a quiet corner, pull out a book, and read until lunch was over. If I heard footsteps coming, I leapt to my feet and walked purposefully down the hall, as if I had somewhere to be.

But at Columbia, I figured, the students would be nerdier, so on a relative basis I might actually be cool.

I lived in a two-room suite with a shared bathroom, but the

two a cappella singers who shared the other room were rarely there. I started spending time in the small lounge at the end of the hall. I'd sit there, folding laundry or reading a book, hoping to meet people.

"In the lounge again, eh Sam?" people would yell down the hall. They'd laugh, then go into their rooms. By the end of the first month, I hadn't made a single friend and was lonelier than I'd ever been.

One day I was talking to a scrawny, quiet guy who lived down the hall from me, and I told him I was good at shooting pool. He said, "My roommate Edward plays pool; you should meet him."

I was nervous but so desperate for a friend that I marched into the room they shared. Edward was standing at the window.

"I hear you play pool," I said. "Any good?"

"Better than you," he said.

The subway ride to Amsterdam Billiards was awkward, but at the pool table, after a few beers, we loosened up. Edward was sarcastic and hilarious, and I spent the evening doubled over with laughter.

Edward was a night owl, the kind only college schedules permit. It was not unusual for him to go to sleep at dawn and wake at four in the afternoon. Nights found us in my room, me sitting in bed, him with a chair pulled up, playing cards. Hours clipped by; we might play a hundred hands in a night.

For dinner Edward and I would go to JJ's Place, the snack bar across campus where we could charge food to our parents' bill. Edward was thin, but he was an eater. He'd order a bacon cheeseburger, fries, and a Coke. I'd get something healthier—a turkey burger or a chicken sandwich. I was worried about making weight, even though wrestling season hadn't started yet. I was trying to cut to 140 pounds, 5 pounds *lighter* than I had wrestled in high school. I figured that since

I wasn't really skilled enough to be a college wrestler, I should wrestle the smallest guys possible.

Sometimes I'd badger Edward into buying pitchers of Rolling Rock at The West End, a dive bar across the street from campus ("Where Columbia drinks its first beer!" their tee shirts read). We'd sit at the bar, and I'd show off for Edward by staring menacingly at other guys in the bar until they looked away. After three or four pitchers, we'd stumble home, laughing.

Soon we were drinking every night.

It's tough to lose weight as a daily beer drinker. I'd wake up hungover, with a vague memory of having eaten cookies. After those nights I'd vow not to get drunk again. Then, after I was drunk again, I'd vow not to eat while drunk again. But I always would. So I tried something new. When I got home from the bars, I started sticking my finger down my throat.

By throwing up, I could drink and eat all I wanted—two pitchers of beer, then pancakes, scrambled eggs, sausage, and a milk shake from the diner on the way home—and feel fine the next day. I felt like I'd discovered a magic trick. As I started to do it more and more, I learned some things. Pizza is one of the hardest things to throw up because the dough is so dense. It's like vomiting up rocks. Milk makes everything easier; throwing up ice cream actually feels sort of pleasant. I began to perfect my technique. I put toilet paper in the water so no one could hear the splash. I wiped down the bowl quickly and efficiently. I puked right before taking a shower, so the bathroom would smell soapy.

Now, at JJ's Place, I ate more than Edward. I tried to be casual about it. Edward ordered a bacon cheeseburger; I ordered a double bacon cheeseburger. He got fries; I got cheese fries. I always bought some sort of dessert, a muffin or a cookie, and a large container of chocolate milk. Sometimes I got a full box of Entenmann's cookies. "For us to split," I'd tell Edward and then proceed to eat all but two. I was terrified Edward would suspect, but he never said anything.

The moment we left JJ's Place I started counting the minutes. The longer it took from when I finished eating to when I booted, the more calories I absorbed. It was a race against the clock. To avoid suspicion, I'd hang out with Edward for a while. We'd go back to my room and play cards. "Just a few hands," I'd say. "I need to study."

He always fought me on it. He had the entire night looming and didn't want to be alone. We were each other's only real friends. He'd beg me to play another hand or two.

Things started to get dicey. One night, after barfing in the bathroom, I opened the door and ran smack into my suite mate, Sebastian, standing there with a toothbrush and a towel. I thought I had the suite to myself. He looked irritated.

"What took you so long, man?" he asked.

I hadn't showered and was afraid it smelled.

"Nothing, man, nothing. Just a little sick. Sorry about that," I said.

Another night, Edward was in my room playing cards and I couldn't get him to leave. "Okay, last hand," I said. "This is it. I gotta get to sleep."

"Stop," he said. "You don't even have class tomorrow."

I had in my belly a Philly cheesesteak, curly fries, a chocolate-chip scone, and a quart of chocolate milk. There was a ticking bomb in my stomach. I played another hand.

"Alright, bro, I'm tired," I said. "Last one."

"Stop," he said. "You're fine. *Five* more." I was afraid if I pushed him, Edward would sense something amiss. I tried to appear calm while my mind broke into full-blown panic. *You can't afford this. You'll gain two or three pounds.* I couldn't focus on the cards. Minutes flew by. We'd eaten over an hour ago. I didn't even feel full anymore—the food was already digesting. Edward was giving me weird looks. *Fuck.*

The staccato thoughts reached a crescendo; it felt like my head might short out like an overstuffed electrical socket. I tried to will Edward to leave, but he just lit another cigarette and blew out perfect smoke rings, like he didn't have a care in the world.

So I did the only thing I could do. I resigned myself to the situation. I decided I wasn't going to hurl that night. It would build credibility, I told myself. I dealt another round of cards and settled in. I felt gross and resentful, but I knew I'd made the right decision. I was protecting my secret.

When wrestling practice started, I was clearly the worst wrestler on the team. *But at least I was skinny.* At the first tournament of the year, the Ivy League Invitational, my first match was against a Harvard wrestler ranked third in the nation. He pinned me in forty-five seconds. In my second match, the captain of Princeton's team ripped my right shoulder out of its socket, and I was out for the season.

I told myself I didn't need to throw up anymore, that my weight didn't matter, but I couldn't stop. I'd go to JJ's Place determined to order a healthy meal, but I'd find myself grabbing a box of cookies, several baked goods, and, of course, milk. I'd eat hurriedly in the dark back booth. Once the food was inside me, I'd start imagining the calories becoming love handles. I'd feel an uncontrollable urge to purge and I'd rush back to my bathroom and lock the door. Soon I was upchucking at least once a day, sometimes two or three times. I knew it wasn't sustainable, yet I felt powerless to stop it.

One day I was watching TV in the lounge with Edward, my neighbor Sabrina, and a vegan hippie named Jessica. Jessica and I started arguing about what channel to watch, and rather quickly it got heated. "You're such a bitch," I said.

"At least I don't throw up every meal," she retorted.

I couldn't speak. All my defense mechanisms—my sarcasm, my stoicism, my ability to laugh things off—were neutralized. I gaped. I was ashamed. I stood and walked into my room.

Edward came in a few minutes later.

"Are you all right, man?"

I looked up at him with tears in my eyes.

"I don't think so," I said. I felt diseased. For the first time, I understood that something inside me was broken.

I was too embarrassed to stay around campus, so I called Ben and asked if I could come visit. He was having a tough freshman year, too—he'd already gotten in several fistfights— and was happy to hear I was coming up. That night Edward and I boarded the bus to Ithaca, a six-hour ride. Edward was excited to meet Ben—I'd often bragged about how smart and tough Ben was—and peppered me with questions. "Who is older? Can you read each other's minds?" Two hours into the drive, he asked, "Have you ever hooked up with the same girl?"

I was quiet. Edward sensed a story. "What happened?" he pressed.

I knew I shouldn't tell him. Emma and I had managed to keep our tryst under wraps for two years. But in truth, I was dying to tell someone. And I didn't like the way Edward's eyes lit up when I talked about how smart Ben was. I told him the whole story.

When Edward and I got off the bus, Ben was waiting. I introduced Edward, and Ben introduced his new girlfriend, Jen. Ben also introduced a skinny, fresh-faced girl from Rochester named Kirsten Thompson. She was all arms and legs, with frizzy hair that exploded out of her head like an Afro, and clearly shy. I liked her immediately.

The first night, Kirsten and I exchanged looks from opposite sides of the group. The next night, we talked quietly on the perimeter. During a snowball fight, I tackled her. Later that night, I kissed her.

She had a roommate, so we couldn't be alone in her room.

Instead, I pushed two couches in the lounge together to make a sort of bed. Anyone could walk by, so we didn't hook up. We talked, then fell asleep in each other's arms. I slept for fourteen hours. In the morning, Kirsten and I went for breakfast.

I didn't want to return to Columbia. I felt safe with Ben. And Kirsten seemed a gift from God. Edward agreed to skip classes for a week to stay at Cornell.

A few nights later we went out to Ben's favorite drinking spot, an old Irish pub called Rulloff's. I stood at the bar with Kirsten and Jen, while Edward and Ben floated off to a table. An hour later, I looked over to see Ben and Edward engaged in intense conversation. As I walked to the bathroom, I wondered what they were talking about.

When I came out, Ben was gone. Edward's head was in his hands. I walked to the table and sat down.

"Where's Ben?" I asked.

Edward kept his head in his hands. He seemed very drunk. Suddenly, I knew.

"You told him about Emma," I said.

Edward's head dropped deeper into his hands. I stared at him, dumbfounded.

"What could you possibly have been thinking?" I said. I called Ben from a pay phone. He didn't pick up. I kept dialing. Ten minutes later his girlfriend answered. "Ben wants you to leave," she said. "He's in my room, so you can pick up your stuff from his room and go."

It was two in the morning. Edward and I fetched our luggage and stood silently in the Ithaca cold until the 4:00 a.m. Short Line bus arrived. As we settled into our seats, Edward's eyes continued to seek mine in apology. I ignored him. I looked straight ahead and thought about Kirsten. I hadn't even said good-bye. I knew I might never see her again. I knew it would be years before Ben forgave me.

CHAPTER 8

The Boy with the Dragon Tattoo

◘

After freshman year of college, Ben stayed at Cornell, but I went home for the summer. It would be the last time I ever went home.

During second semester, I'd befriended another freshman wrestler, a heavyweight named Francisco who loved to party. We'd become drinking buddies, then drug buddies. I now smoked weed every day. I was still throwing up, but not as much. I'd used a combination of willpower and sleeping pills to cut back. Hungry at night, instead of eating, I'd take two Valiums to knock me out. But I still yacked from time to time. The second day of the summer, home alone, I ordered an extra-large cheese-in-the-crust pepperoni pizza and two dozen chicken wings, ate them, and then vomited in the toilet.

One night I was smoking a joint in the backyard when Dad came out. He looked at me, looked at the joint, and then asked if he could have a drag. I looked up at him in surprise.

"You remember how your friend Nate Robertson used to stop by all the time while you were in high school?" he asked. I nodded.

"He was selling me pot," Dad said.

I felt a dull ache in my chest as I registered that Dad and my friend had kept a secret from me for years. But I didn't protest. I didn't want Dad to get mad, go inside. Sometimes it felt like the price of being with him was getting my feelings hurt.

Dad didn't talk to me like a son. More like a fishing buddy. The summer before, when I worked for Dad's public relations firm, he'd told me during one of our drives home that Stacy, an attractive young woman he'd hired to answer phones, sometimes gave her boyfriend "Altoid blow jobs," where she'd put two Altoids in her mouth and then go down on him.

"It's an amazing feeling," Dad said. "Apparently."

I'd known it was weird for Dad to tell me that and to be talking to Stacy about stuff like that. But I loved that he was giving me a peek into a world he kept hidden from the rest of our family. Dad and I had an unspoken understanding—I'd stolen his porn magazines for years, and he never said a word. I smiled conspiratorially and never looked at Stacy the same way again.

I got a job as a bicycle messenger on the Disney Studios lot. It was a good job—fresh air, riding a bike all day. But there was one problem—our family only had two cars, which meant I had to carpool with Mom. I would drop her off at the clinic, then drive to Disney. After work I'd pick her up and drive her home.

Mom had always been late. Growing up, it wasn't unusual for Ben and I to be kicking dirt on the baseball diamond, the stadium and parking lot empty, an hour after all the other kids had gone home.

Each morning I'd be standing at the front door. "Mom, we were supposed to leave ten minutes ago."

"Almost ready," she'd yell back.

After work it was even worse. I'd call her as I was leaving Disney and ask her to meet me outside. When I arrived, there'd be no sign of her. I'd wait in the car, stewing.

When she got in the car I'd say, "Mom, I've been waiting

twenty minutes!" I tried to keep my voice calm, but when I finished I'd be shaking. She'd say one of her patients took longer than expected. We'd ride home in a toxic silence.

One night, I was in the living room reading, and I could hear Mom and Dad arguing in their bedroom. Mom was trying to sleep. Dad wouldn't get off his cell phone.

"Tony, can you please be quiet?" she said. He didn't answer her.

A few minutes later, Mom tried again. "Tony, I'm trying to sleep," she said. I could hear the anger in her voice.

"Leave me the fuck alone, Linda," Dad spat back.

"Go talk somewhere else!" Mom barked.

Dad ignored her. For a few seconds we listened to him talk into the phone.

"Fuck you, Tony," Mom suddenly shouted. The bed creaked. I imagined her turning away from him, enraged.

I hunched over in anticipation. I knew Dad was going to retaliate—I just wasn't sure how. He hung up the phone. For a moment there was silence. Then the bed creaked as Dad stood up. A few seconds later, he charged past me into the kitchen. I heard the freezer open and ice cubes hitting the bottom of a pitcher. He stormed past me going the other way, this time carrying a pitcher of ice water. He walked over to Mom's side of the bed and pulled the covers off her. When he dumped the pitcher of ice water on her, she screamed. I'd never heard anything like that scream before. It was animalistic.

When they fought, I'd always sided with Dad. But hearing him douse her, warm in bed, with freezing water was the single worst thing I'd ever witnessed. I wanted to comfort her, but I didn't.

For several days, I went out of my way to be kind to Mom. But she kept making me late to work, and by the end of the week my resentment had returned. On Friday, I called her after work and said I'd pick her up in ten minutes and would really appreciate if she were downstairs when I arrived. She said she would be.

When I got there, she was nowhere to be seen. I called her number. When I got her voice mail, I became furious. I called back three times before she finally picked up.

"Sam," she said, exasperated, "I'm coming down."

"You said you'd be waiting," I said tersely.

"Oh fuck off," she said.

Suddenly, I was angrier than I'd ever been. Blood pounded through my temples. She *never* respected my time. She *always* put herself first. How *dare* she treat me like that. By the time she walked out, twenty minutes later, I was a boiling kettle. As soon as she got in, I jammed the accelerator, and the Mazda minivan shot off down the road. As she fastened her seat belt, I let loose the torrent of words that had built up inside me.

"Mom, I've had enough of your shit," I said. "I'm sick of always waiting for you. I'm sick of you wasting my time. I'm sick of all of it. This is the last time that happens."

As I talked, she was silent. I had to keep my eyes on the road, but I kept glancing at her to make sure my words were affecting her. She stared straight ahead, but I could tell by the set of her jaw that she heard every word.

I was looking at the road, about to change lanes, when a clenched fist slugged me in the side of the head.

I looked over at Mom, shocked. She looked like a demon. Her face was bright red, making vivid the white hairs on her chin. Her eyes were wild. Her jaw quivered.

"Mom, what the fuck?" I shouted. "I'm driving!"

She turned in her seat so that she was facing me directly. Wham! Wham! Wham! She unleashed a series of punches. We were in the middle of traffic going about forty miles an hour, so I had to keep my eyes on the road. I hunched my shoulders to my ears and raised my right hand to block her punches. One hit me square in the neck. One landed on the meat of my upper arm. She hit me on the top of my head.

My rage was gone, and I was simply terrified. Mom didn't seem to care if she killed us both. The car next to me honked as I faded into its lane. I veered back into my lane. Mom's blows slowed. Her chest was heaving with exhaustion. There was a break in the traffic, and I yanked the wheel to the right and pulled us off the road.

"Mom!" I screamed.

That attack was beyond anything she'd ever done. I started crying. "Mom," I begged. "Are you gonna let me drive us home? Will you promise not to hit me while I'm driving?"

She didn't say anything. With tears streaming down my face, I pulled back onto the road. We had a fifteen-minute drive ahead of us, most of it on the freeway. I was scared she was going to start hitting me again. But what came next was even worse. Mom had gone somewhere deep inside herself. When she spoke, it was in a voice I'd never heard before.

"You are an ungrateful shit," she said, "just like your father. You are a terrible son, a terrible person. I wish you'd never been born."

For the next fifteen minutes she didn't stop talking. She listed all the things she hated about me, the ways I'd let her down. At first I responded with sarcastic protestations. "Yeah, really, Mom? That's really what you think of your own son?" But mostly I stayed quiet and listened as my mom told me how much she detested me.

When we pulled up to the house, I jumped out of the car and rushed across the lawn. Dad opened the front door. When I saw him, I started sobbing.

"What happened?" he said.

"Mom kept punching me while I was driving," I said. "And then spent the whole drive home telling me how much she hated me." I could hardly breathe.

He looked stricken. More than anything I wanted him to stand up for me. *Do something. Protect me.*

"I'm sorry," he said.

Which meant he wasn't going to do anything. Mom had gotten into the driver's seat and I heard her peel away. I went into my room and lay on my bed, exhausted. I felt like a satellite adrift in deep space, connected to nothing, cold and alone.

In the last week of summer, Edward came out to visit me, and Ben came home for a week. I was anxious about us all being together, but Ben ignored us, kept to himself.

That Friday Edward and I decided to go to a party across town. We were waiting to be picked up by some guys I knew from high school when, at the last minute, Ben said he was coming. He sat in the backseat, silent, looking out the window. I think he just needed to get drunk.

At the party we went our separate ways. A few hours later I was very drunk when I saw Ben getting in an argument. The guy stepped toward Ben; Ben head butted him in the face. I rushed in to help, but someone pushed me and I toppled backwards over a bush.

By the time I got up, Ben was being pushed back toward a gate at the rear of the backyard by people trying to stop the fight from escalating. Others were trying to calm the friends of the guy Ben had head butted. I ran to Ben, and he and I were suddenly pushed through the wooden gate, which slammed closed behind us.

We found ourselves in an alley that ran behind the house. Edward had come out of the gate before us, and was relieved to see we'd made it out safely. But Ben was screaming taunts over the fence, trying to open the gate to get back in.

"What are you doing, dude?" I hissed. "Let's get the fuck out of here."

"Fuck them," Ben said. The shouts behind the fence were

growing louder, and I could hear people frantically trying to quell the fury of what now sounded like a mob.

"There are like thirty guys back there," I said. I looked to Edward for support, but he was fading into the shadows of the hedge next to the street.

"I don't care how many there are," Ben said and then ripped off his shirt. His thick muscles rippled under the red-and-green dragon tattoo that covered his right arm from elbow to shoulder. He'd gotten that tattoo right before college, and for the first time I saw it as more than just a symbol of toughness. Fighting thirty guys wasn't tough—it was crazy.

The gate swung open and a cadre of drunk, angry men streamed out.

The first three went for Ben, and I saw him snap back the leader's head with a left jab to the chin. The next four guys through the gate went after me, and I started backpedaling as I threw punches to keep them at bay.

My punches were connecting, and I kept my feet moving. I wasn't getting hit too hard, but then a punch connected with my temple, and I went down but scrambled to my feet before anyone could get ahold of me.

I heard tires screech behind me, and I glanced back and saw the Nissan Pathfinder we'd arrived in lurch to a stop, perpendicular across the street. The back door flew open, and the guys we came with screamed for us to get in the car. Edward and I scrambled in. Then I looked for Ben, and I'll never forget what I saw.

He was moving backwards, with five guys after him. There was one guy in the lead, and all of a sudden Ben leaned in and hit him with a hard left hook to the body. He must have hit a kidney, because all of a sudden the guy collapsed to his knees and dropped his hands. And without even pausing, Ben pivoted on his left foot, putting all his weight into it, and slugged the guy in the temple with his left fist. A sharp crack rang out, like wood being split.

The other guys pulled up short. The brutality of the punch stopped them in their tracks. Ben dropped his hands, stood up tall, and started walking toward them.

"Ben!" I screamed. "Get in the car."

He looked back at me, and it was as if I had woken him from a dream. He looked at the guys, who were still backing away, looked down at the guy on the ground, and then hustled over to the car. The door slammed, tires squealed, and we were gone.

CHAPTER 9

The Burglary

◻

Six months later, I stood on the cobblestone path that bisected Columbia University. It was Christmas 1999—halfway through my sophomore year. I'd remained in New York over the break, because I didn't want to go home. The sky was gray, drizzling. My jacket was thin so I jammed my hands into my pockets and hunched my shoulders to my ears.

I saw Neo in the distance, crossing Broadway from the west, wearing a hat and big pants, boots, and a puffy jacket. He was a Cuban from Florida, and he never looked comfortable in the New York cold. He wrestled at 119 pounds and was tall and lanky, all arms and legs, unusual for that weight class. When opponents would shoot in, he would sprawl and it was like a bug caught in a spider's net. They would wriggle, and Neo would adjust. They would strain, and he would tilt. Before they knew it, they were trapped, and he was on top with a two-point take-down. Once he got on top, he stayed there. He was one of the best leg riders I ever saw. He'd started on varsity as a freshman.

I, on the other hand, hadn't. After being injured for most of freshman year, I got cut from the team. I wasn't surprised—I was smoking weed and taking Valium daily and had put on twenty pounds after I stopped throwing up, having replaced bulimia with new addictions.

As soon as I was cut from the team, I started taking steroids. Many Columbia wrestlers took them during the season, but I hadn't wanted to risk getting caught. But now that I was off the team, there was no chance of an NCAA drug test. Neo wanted to know why I wanted to take steroids if I wasn't going to compete. I told him the truth—I just wanted to feel bigger, stronger, more powerful.

I'd been picking up the steroid pills from Neo's suite, where many of the other wrestlers hung out. In an effort to impress them, I told them I'd figured out a way to break into any dorm room on campus. They laughed and said I'd never do it. Neo was the leader of that group. He said I didn't have the balls to go through with it.

He was wrong.

Neo walked up to me and nodded, and we set off toward the security office where students who have locked themselves out of their dorm rooms can retrieve a replacement key.

"Do you want me to go in with you?" he said.

"It's better if I'm alone," I said. I left him leaning against a wall, his cap low over his face, water dripping off the tightly curved bill. I walked into the dark, dry hall. The security guard was at the counter.

"I locked my keys in my room," I said.

"ID?"

"Locked my wallet in my room, too," I said.

He matched my gaze for a beat. My stomach tensed. Then he sighed, eased off his stool, and turned toward the file cabinets on the back wall.

"Room number?" he called over his shoulder. With his back to me I didn't need to hold my face so tight, and my lip quivered with fear.

"1109," I said.

"Name?" he called.

"Randy Moreland," I said.

Randy was a drug dealer who lived in the room next to me. His two best friends were Percy, the tallest hippie I'd ever seen, and Jim, who was soft, quiet, and always wore a huge smile on his face. They spent nearly every night in his room, rolling joints, passing pipes, even inhaling through a gas mask. I really liked Jim, wanted to become friends with him. But I didn't know how.

I'd started buying weed from Randy earlier in the semester and had been invited to smoke with him a few times. Randy kept his stash in a huge jar, and for me he'd carefully pick out a few buds and weigh them to the decimal. For his friends, he'd stick his whole hand into the jar, forearm deep, and pull out a fistful, buds raining down on his desk. Percy and Jim would smile and lean back with the easy comfort of close friends.

I overheard Randy tell Percy he could buy Ecstasy cheap in bulk: $17 a pill, for fifty pills. It'd take him less than a month to sell them all at $25 each, he said. I wanted so much to be a part of this group, to be invited to every session like Jim and Percy. So I offered to fund the deal. I was expecting a check from the government, a Pell Grant that student athletes receive. I was supposed to sign it over to my dad, but I'd just tell him there was a delay.

Randy would sell the pills and split the profits with me. But once I got a taste for Ecstasy, all I wanted was more. When I was "rolling," I was comfortable and charming in a way I'd never been before. Walking into The West End was like walking into Cheers. I'd find myself in conversations with women I'd stared at for weeks but hadn't found the courage to approach. Sometimes I'd even get their numbers.

I started asking Randy for pills two or three times a week, telling him to take it out of my end. After a while he started saying no, that I was swallowing all the profits. One day he got fed up.

"You don't have any discipline, dude," he said. "After this batch, we're done."

I felt like I'd been slapped. That night I heard him, Percy, and Jim talking in Randy's room. Then I heard my name, and they all laughed.

The security guard waded through the files. When he got close, he started going one by one. Finally, he pulled out a manila envelope from a folder and removed the key from inside. He set the key on the counter and put a form down for me to fill out.

I started with NAME, writing each letter of Randy's name slowly, then ROOM NUMBER, DORM, PHONE EXTENSION, SOCIAL SECURITY NUMBER. Halfway through the last line, I realized I'd been filling in *my* social security number. *Idiot!*

I slid the paper across the smooth counter. He picked it up and looked at it. My jaw tensed. He looked up at me, then down at the key. "Thanks," I mumbled. I turned around and tried to walk slowly but found myself walking very fast.

I flew by Neo. Out of the corner of my eye I saw him start up and jolt after me, scrambling to catch up. "What the fuck, man? What the fuck happened?" he said.

"I . . . I . . . I messed up."

"What?"

"They asked for *his* social security number, but I wrote in mine. Only four or five numbers."

"Fuck," he said.

"I doubt they'll catch it," I said.

Neo stopped. "Should we even do this, dude?" he asked.

I didn't break my stride. It would have been a good question for someone else. But I *had* to do it. Randy had made me feel small, and he was going to pay. And in the process, I'd earn Neo's respect.

"Don't be a pussy," I said.

Neo and I walked through the front doors of my dorm,

took the elevator up, then walked down the long hallway to my room. Randy's room sat to the right of mine. In my room, Neo took a pillowcase from one of my pillows. I pulled a suitcase with wheels from the closet.

"See if anyone's out there," I said.

He carefully opened the door. "It's clear," he said.

He held the door as I pulled the suitcase into the hall. My hands felt thick, clumsy, and I fumbled with the key. When I finally opened it, we stepped inside. The door closed behind us with a click, which echoed in the stillness of someone else's private space.

I opened the closet and reached up to the top shelf, where I'd seen Randy store his drugs and money. Only clothes. We searched his room but there wasn't much: some CDs, a video game system, and a three-foot bong. I found a large ball of resin he'd been collecting. Pot leaves a residue, and if you collect it by scraping the bowl after smoking, you can build up a dense, sticky ball that you can smoke; it lasts a long time and sparks and crackles and gives a different high. A resin ball is a prized commodity among serious smokers; it's earned, not bought.

I zipped up the suitcase, and we hustled back into my room. I lay down on my twin bed. There was an inflatable armchair next to the bed, one of those ridiculous pieces of furniture only found in dorm rooms. It squeaked as Neo lowered himself into it. We hadn't been settled for more than two minutes when we heard steps coming down the hall. We froze.

The light changed under the door; a shadow fell, grew. The steps paused, right in front of my door. It was as if the person were in the room with us. Then a key slid into the lock on Randy's door.

We heard the door swing open and held our breath. We didn't have to wait long. Randy's shout exploded from the silence like gunfire. "I'VE BEEN ROBBED! OH NO!

FUCK! FUCK! THEY TOOK THE BONG. THEY TOOK MY FUCKING BONG!"

We heard him rip the phone off the cradle. "Dude. I've been robbed ... yeah ... robbed. They took, let's see, they took my bong, my CDs ..." The drawer to his desk was ripped open. "THEY TOOK MY FUCKING RESIN BALL. WHO THE FUCK WOULD STEAL A RESIN BALL? No, man, no one is here. The building is fucking empty."

Just then, Neo shifted and the inflatable chair squeaked.

"Hold on a second," Randy said.

We heard him stride into the hallway. As he moved to my door, the steps grew louder, heavier. All of a sudden, fists hammered the thin wooden door; it quaked in its frame. My body, which was already tight, clenched even tighter and went cold.

"SAM. SAM," Randy yelled. "SAM, ARE YOU THERE?"

Neo and I were statues. I clenched my teeth and didn't breathe.

Randy pounded again and again, then gave up. He went back into his room, gathered some stuff, and then left. His steps faded down the hall. We were quiet until the elevator bell dinged and the doors opened and closed.

"Holy shit," Neo whispered.

Blood pounded through my temples. "Let's get out of here," I said.

As we rode down the elevator, I imagined Randy at the bottom with a phalanx of cops, a K9 dog. The doors opened. No one was there. Neo and I hustled past the security guard, hats pulled low, out into the cold air.

CHAPTER 10

ON24

◻

A month after I broke into Randy's room, I was sum-moned to the Columbia Security Department. The head of security, a mountain of a man, pointed to the social security line on the form I'd forged to get Randy's key. He said I could either admit my guilt, in which case they'd handle the matter internally, or I could deny it, in which case they'd turn over the evidence to the NYPD. I stared defiantly at him for a moment and then burst into tears.

Two days later I was suspended from Columbia for a se-mester. As I walked down the hall toward my dorm room to pack up my stuff, Randy emerged from his room. I hoped he'd try to fight me; I could be gracious. Instead he looked hurt and said, "I can't believe you did that, man." I wanted to crawl inside myself.

"I'm sorry," I mumbled.

That afternoon I sat on one of the other wrestlers' beds and called Dad.

"You fucking idiot," he hissed. A cold wind blew through my body.

I didn't want to go home, so I rented a tiny room in an apartment near campus. Whenever I passed other students, I'd keep my eyes glued to the sidewalk. I couldn't bear the thought of running into people I knew, seeing their judgment, feeling my shame.

I found an internship at a two-man Internet start-up called Virtual Stock Exchange that paid $8 an hour. That job was my life raft—my bosses didn't know what I'd done, so at work I could hold my head up. I started to fantasize about the story of a boy kicked out of college who joins a start-up and becomes a millionaire. I imagined pulling up to campus in a Porsche.

The office was a large, single room, and my bosses coded silently all day long. My job was to forge partnerships with other websites, and to do that I needed to send out hundreds of e-mails per day. I started taking Ritalin in the afternoons to help me finish work strong. After work I'd come home and drink a bottle of wine. After a while, that wasn't enough to put me to sleep, so I started topping off with NyQuil.

There was only one person I could stand being around: another Columbia student named Elyn Walker, who was in as much trouble as I was. Elyn, a thin girl from Michigan with short, sandy-blond hair, had been arrested with twelve wax-paper packets of heroin. Columbia suggested she take some time off. She'd rented a tiny room on 120th and Amsterdam, and we'd stay there all weekend, me doing coke, her doing heroin *and* coke. Sometimes we'd have sex. After, we'd go to the corner bodega and Elyn would get Diet Coke and an extra-large Tootsie Roll. Dinner.

Aside from the drugs and the sex, the reason I loved being with Elyn was because she was the only person in the world I didn't have to hide from. A few weeks after we met, she told me she was bulimic, and I told her I'd been, too, and after that we had no secrets. She was my refuge.

One day at work I came across a beautifully curated website with a blue-and-yellow logo that read "ON24." I saw an address in San Francisco. I clicked on the Career Opportunities link. They were looking for someone to do business development—the requirements were a college degree and at least three years' experience. I typed an e-mail to the CEO:

I'm 19 and in college, but I can do this job.

I said I'd taken time off from Columbia to participate in the Internet boom. Within an hour the CEO, Sharat Sharan, e-mailed me and asked if I was available for a call that Friday.

That Thursday night, Elyn came over to my apartment. When she arrived, she pulled a tiny Ziploc bag out of her pocket. It was filled with powder the color of brown sugar—heroin. I'd asked her to bring some for me.

She sprinkled some powder into a pipe. I smoked it, then sat down on the bed. I finally understood what the big deal was about heroin. It was like I was wrapped in the toastiest blanket in the world, wearing thick slippers, sipping hot cocoa in front of a roaring fire. Comfortable. Safe. Content. I'd never felt like that before.

I lay in bed and Elyn pulled up a chair. I nodded off. When I came to, I shook Elyn and she sprinkled more heroin on top of the weed in my pipe and I smoked it. We stayed there all night, waking intermittently, but mostly off in our nods.

When I woke, it was light out. The clock read 10:00 a.m. I was already two hours late to work. I walked to the bathroom and splashed water on my face. Then I sat on the edge of the bed and dialed the number Sharat had given me.

He came on the line and asked about my experience at VSE. The residue of heroin in my blood left me calm and relaxed, and I answered his questions slowly and fully. He listened for a while and then, satisfied, started telling me about ON24. He said he wanted to fly me out to San Francisco to interview but didn't want to waste the money if I wasn't absolutely sure I was willing to move out there. I smiled, looking at Elyn in her tight tee shirt and big jeans passed out on a folding chair, her leg up on the bed and her left arm dangling straight down, a needle sticking out of the vein in her arm.

"Yes," I said. "I'm ready to leave New York."

Two weeks later, I sat across from Sharat. He slid a piece of paper toward me. I picked it up: $30,000 per year, three thousand stock options. If you broke it down by hour, it was close to minimum wage. But to me, $30,000 was a fortune. Plus, those stock options could be worth millions if ON24 did an IPO.

I moved into a ground-floor studio apartment I found on the Internet, four blocks from the office. Four blocks in the wrong direction, it turned out. The drab, gray apartment building sat smack in the center of the Tenderloin, a notoriously seedy neighborhood littered with strip clubs, XXX theaters, liquor stores, and a dimly lit pool hall.

I worked with the laser focus of a zealot. Ritalin—which I'd begun ordering online from a pharmacy in Mexico— helped. When I'd start to flag in the afternoon, I'd head to the bathroom, a single-seater with a fragile slide-bolt lock. I pulled my pants down and sat on the toilet. I took a blue plastic pill crusher and a foil sheet of pills out of my pocket, ejected one into the crusher, and rotated it two or three times until the pill became fine powder. I rolled a dollar bill from my wallet into a tube and snorted the pile of powder.

My armpits immediately started sweating, and most times I'd have to go to the bathroom, which was pretty convenient. After I finished I put everything back in my pocket, flushed, and went to the mirror to wash my hands and splash water on my now-hot face. I checked my nostrils for residue, then walked back down the hall, ready to fire off a thousand e-mails. I worked furiously for hours, barely looking up when people passed on their way out for the night. It'd be eight or nine at night, the office would be empty, and I'd still be grinding my teeth and firing off e-mails.

I was building a network of partner sites that would display ON24's content and generate advertising revenue. The size of the network was critical, and Sharat set ambitious goals. I handled conference calls myself. At first I stumbled over words and would scurry into Sharat's office with questions. But after a dozen calls, I knew the answers, found my pacing. It's amazing how smooth something can sound once you say it a hundred times. Ten partner sites became a hundred. At the company meeting each week Sharat began to ask me for updates on new deals. I would stammer and flush, but afterward I'd be proud.

Late at night, I'd stand up from my desk, put on a jacket, lock the office door, and step into the night. Ritalin screws up your body temperature; in the office, I couldn't stop sweating, but in the cool San Francisco night I was freezing, even with my jacket on. I always listened to Tupac on the walk home; it made me feel aggressive, my angry face a protective shield against the bums and dealers. At home I'd drink NyQuil and a forty-ounce Bud Light, and my shoulders would relax as warmth spread through my body.

Sometimes at lunch, I hustled a mile into the Mission District and through the door of a squat, dingy building, an underground kickboxing gym filled with the sounds of knees hitting bags and fists hitting heads. I changed into shorts, wrapped my hands, and worked myself until sweat dripped off me like a rain gutter. Then I showered, changed back into my button-down shirt and glasses, and headed back to the office.

I had no friends and no girlfriends. Sometimes I went to bars, hoping to meet a woman. I'd grab a stool, order a drink, and look around, trying to catch someone's eye. I never met anyone. After a while I felt foolish and sad, and I'd leave, embarrassed.

In those first months, I talked to Dad on the phone every day. I'd call and ask him for business advice. I'd tell him about the deals I was signing, how big the network was growing. One night I came home to find my ground-floor window smashed, my apartment robbed. I called my dad and asked him to pay for a hotel that night because I was scared and the window wouldn't be fixed till the next morning. It wasn't that I needed the money—I actually had a couple hundred in the bank. I just wanted him to take care of me, and thought that this time he wouldn't be able to say no.

"Too expensive," he said. "They likely won't come back."

A few weeks later, my friend Sabrina, who played tennis for Columbia, drove up from Santa Cruz to visit me. She brought a freshman teammate with her. Sloane Taylor's blond hair cascaded down her back. She had caramel skin, full lips, and a tight figure. She walked into my studio apartment like she was starring in a movie.

From the moment I saw her I wanted her. I reached for a handshake; she laughed delightedly, threw her arms around my neck, kissed my throat, and asked if I had any pot. Sloane was way out of my league, the class of women I'd always coveted but never got—cheerleaders in junior high, prom queens in high school.

They wanted to party. I took them to a club in the Tenderloin. Sloane smiled when I pressed a Ritalin into her palm, but when I tried to dance with her, she'd move away. We all took a 4:00 a.m. swim in the pool in my apartment complex. When we got back to my room, Sloane leaned in to whisper something in my ear.

"Do you have a Valium?" she asked. I fetched two and took one myself. We fell asleep at dawn. When I woke up later that morning, she was gone.

A month later, I called Dad to tell him about a new deal I'd signed. I thought he'd be proud of me, but instead he seemed irritated. "You are building this company," he said. "You need to get compensated for it." He seemed almost angry, as if *he* were being slighted. The previous week, the deal to sell his company had fallen through.

I brushed him off, but the next day my gaze lingered suspiciously on my coworkers, wondering how many stock options *they* had been granted. Soon it was all I could think about. I seethed during meetings, silently disparaging my better-compensated coworkers. After a few weeks, I was fed up. I strode into Sharat's office.

"What is it, Sam?"

"I want to talk about changing my compensation structure," I belted out.

He sat back in his chair. "Again?" he said. I'd asked for a raise a few months after I arrived.

I may be twenty, I thought, *but I am building this firm.* I'd heard people refer to me as Sharat's protégé. What was I doing with just three thousand stock options?

Sharat looked miffed. "Sam, I understand you are impatient, and in some sense that's good. But these things take time. Keep your head down and things will work out. You can't just tell people how valuable you are; you need to let them discover it themselves."

But that was bullshit. No one ever suddenly discovered my value. I'd had to scratch and claw for recognition my whole life.

I started again, but he cut me off with a wave.

"Okay, Sam. You have to agree not to talk to me about this again for a year. A full year, okay? Now, what do you want?"

I hurried into the hallway, validated, but also aware of a splinter of hesitation. I had gotten exactly what I wanted, but could I have gotten more? I pushed the thought aside and called Dad.

"He went for it," I said. "Sixty thousand dollars a year, and a thousand more options."

"Good for you," Dad said. My chest filled with pride.

"They are still getting a bargain at sixty thousand dollars," he continued. My shoulders sagged. As I listened to the speech I'd heard Dad give a hundred times, Sharat walked out of his office and into the hallway. He saw me on the phone and stopped. I'd told him how often I talked on the phone with my father. Sharat looked thoughtful, like he was deciding whether to speak.

"Your dad may not be the best source of guidance for you, Sam," said Sharat. "It might be time for you to start making your own decisions."

And he strode off down the hallway.

A few months later I flew out to Minnesota to visit Elyn. She'd gone to rehab at Hazelden and was now living nearby in a halfway house. She was waiting for me at the airport gate. The first thought through my mind was, "Good God, what *happened* to you?"

Quitting heroin and controlling her bulimia is what happened. She was at least thirty pounds heavier. Her hair had lost its blond highlights and was now just plain brown. I'd been attracted to her heroin chic, hot-mess aesthetic. Now that she was healthy, those feelings were gone. I forced my face into a smile.

She took me to an AA meeting. It was in an old clubhouse. There were maybe one hundred people there, many of them teenagers, smoking cigarettes, gulping coffee, talking frantically. I kept my eyes down as Elyn talked to people. Elyn found us seats in the center. I felt trapped.

The meeting started. There were some readings; then a speaker was introduced. He was a big man, construction worker type. He talked about his cocaine abuse. The jobs he'd lost, the people he'd hurt. I'd never heard anyone talk like that, with such honesty. I hung on his every word. He talked about getting sober, what his life was like now.

At the end, he said that talking like this had been really hard for him, because his seven-year-old son was in the audience. But even though he was embarrassed at everything he'd done, how low he'd fallen, he needed to tell the truth. Because when his son was born, he promised himself he'd never lie to him.

A lump formed in my throat, and my eyes welled. I tried to stop them but tears ran down my face. Elyn grabbed my hand. I clenched my teeth and waited for the pain to pass. It was the accountability—a father trying to be a better man for his son. I felt a deep gash across my heart. I looked up at Elyn. She looked back with kind eyes and rubbed my back.

I was relieved when I finally boarded the plane back to San Francisco. After takeoff, I ordered a drink. Then another. I felt better.

CHAPTER 11

Fight Club

◘

Six months later, I convinced a Canadian financial news website to pay ON24 $100,000 for our content, and Sharat gave me a $15,000 bonus. ON24 had grown to over two hundred employees and started construction on a new floor of offices. An IPO seemed imminent.

To celebrate I went to a rave that weekend with a new friend from work, and we ran into two Vietnamese girls who worked at ON24. The girls—Kylie and Eunice—had a baggie filled with Ecstasy. I bought two pills from them. I don't remember much after that. I woke with a vague memory that someone had been angry with me.

The next Friday, I was on a conference call when an e-mail bleeped in my in-box:

> If you do not immediately pay the money you owe to my girlfriend, I will come down to your office and fuck you up. What kind of a person doesn't pay his debts, and to girls? If this is not taken care of today, I am going to fuck you up beyond belief. You have been warned.

My body went cold. I had no idea what he was talking about, but I guessed he must be connected to Kylie and Eunice. When the call ended, I e-mailed them to meet me in a conference room. When they walked in, neither looked me in the eye.

"Um, do you know someone named Duc?" I asked.

They looked at each other nervously. Then Kylie spoke.

"He's my boyfriend."

I glared. "I just received a threatening e-mail from him. Do you have any idea how much trouble you can get in for that? What is he talking about anyway?"

Kylie's eyes flashed. "You owe me eighty dollars, and you haven't paid it all week."

I suddenly recalled the strange looks I'd gotten from them in the hall at work that week. I figured I'd just been rude to them while in a blackout.

"What the fuck?" I said. "Why wouldn't you just tell me that? I don't even *remember*. I could get you fired for this. I can't *believe* I received a threatening e-mail at my desk today. This is a place of business. An *office*!"

I was quaking with anger.

Kylie cut in. "I told him not to. But he said we had to get the money."

"Don't try to dispel the blame," I sneered.

"You better pay," she said. "He can get crazy."

I stiffened. She didn't know it, but her words sealed it. I didn't care about these girls. I didn't care about Duc. But I wouldn't back down. I hadn't backed down from a fight since I beat up Jorge at Camp Fox ten years earlier. I left the room without a word.

I went downstairs to the ATM and got $80, then bought a coffee with a twenty and took the change and put it in my pocket with the three remaining twenties. I summoned the girls to the conference room.

"Here's your money," I said when they arrived. "I would've paid you if you'd asked. I'm only giving you seventy-nine dol-

lars. I'm keeping one dollar. I want you to tell your boyfriend.
If he's unhappy with that, he can come here and talk to me
about it."

I walked out.

I felt like I'd regained some power. But I couldn't stand
the thought of Kylie and Eunice laughing with Duc about
how quickly I'd paid up. I went back to my desk and typed
out an e-mail:

> I don't know who you think you are, but don't ever
> send me threatening e-mails, especially to my work
> address. I didn't realize that I owed the girls money,
> and as soon as I found out I paid them. But because
> of the way you handled this, I kept $1 so you would
> know that I wasn't going to be pushed around. If
> you want the $1, you can come down here to get it.

Furious, I hit Send. In five minutes I got a reply:

> I'll be there at 4 p.m.

It was like I could see it all happening again—the down-
ward spiral—but couldn't stop it. I was an adult, a business-
man on the verge of his big break; I was also that bullied
boy who'd had enough. At 3:45 p.m. I went into an empty
conference room and stared out the window. I didn't want to
lose my job. And I was scared, trembling. But I had a trigger;
Duc had pulled it.

I took the elevator down to the ground floor. I walked
past the security desk and into the daylight and noise of Market Street. I put two quarters into a newspaper machine and
pulled out a *Chronicle* and stood there pretending to read it.
A corporate warrior on a coffee break. My heart pounded in
my chest.

I felt him before I saw him. He was a muscular Asian in a black, puffy jacket, and by the time I saw him he was already in my face. His eyes were two inches from mine.

"Give me my fucking dollar," he said.

I stepped back and put my hands up, placating. "Whoa, guy," I said. "Whoa. Not here. We need to go somewhere we can talk."

"Give me my fucking money," he repeated, pushing into me. "You should have just given them the money. Then you wouldn't have to deal with me."

"I'm looking forward to dealing with you," I growled. "Come with me."

I turned heel and walked into the building. He followed. I walked up to the security desk and quickly wrote down the name Duc on the sign-in sheet. I nodded to the security guard and pointed to the furious gangster next to me as if to say, *This gentleman is with me.* I strode to the elevator and pushed the button.

"Give me my fucking money," Duc said loudly. While I tried to shush him two other office workers came up behind us, waiting for the elevator. I kept my eyes trained on the doors, trying to will Duc not to make a scene. The doors opened. The four of us filed into the elevator. Duc and I stood closest to the door. I pushed 2.

Duc, losing it, turned toward me as the doors shut. "What the fuck?" he said.

I didn't even turn as I spat out, "Not now—wait." When the doors opened, I stepped out quickly, half expecting him to take a swing at me right there. He didn't.

I strode down the hall to the new ON24 offices. They were renovating the space, which was now gutted and empty. Duc followed. I took keys out of my pocket and opened the lock. We stepped through the door into a cavernous room, the skeleton of an office. Massive concrete columns military pressed the ceiling. There were piles of lumber and drywall. The dirty windowpanes admitted only a few rays of light.

I tossed my newspaper on the ground. "Okay," I said, facing Duc. "Now we can talk."

"Give me my fucking money," he said.

"A dollar? You came here for a dollar?" I said, trying to shame him, even though I would've done the same.

"Fuck you," he said.

"Do something then," I taunted.

He did. He reached up to my face, grabbed my glasses, folded them in half, dropped them on the ground, and stepped on them with a crunch. Then he flew at me. I kept my feet apart, kickboxing style, and jabbed him in the face. He came in again. I was taller and had reach. I pivoted and hit him again. My punches felt weak to me, but I could see a red bump swelling over his eye.

He changed tack and tried to tackle me. Which was, it turned out, a mistake. I may not have been a good college wrestler, but I was a good high school wrestler. Against someone with no wrestling experience, it almost wasn't fair. As his momentum started to topple us, I shifted so my left hip was pressed against his right hip, and we were facing the same direction. I reached my left arm behind his back and grabbed his left bicep with my left hand. When we hit the floor, my body trapped his right arm underneath, so now we were pressed together, wriggling on the floor, with both of his arms pinned and my right arm—and my right fist—free.

I started punching him in the face. As he realized the helplessness of his position, he became frantic. His flailing took on an air of desperation. I realized he was terrified.

I stopped. I didn't really want to hurt him; I just didn't want to deal with the self-hatred of backing down.

"Just give up, dude," I said.

He tried to bite my face. I hit him again, as a warning. It

was clear he was trapped, that he'd lost, but he wouldn't give up. He tried to head butt me. I arched my back to keep my head away. As he struggled harder and harder, my hold got tighter and tighter. I punched him in the face again and again.

I got scared. I got scared that he'd never stop, that I'd keep hitting him in the face.

I let him go. I stood up. He stayed on the ground. I pulled a dollar bill from my pocket, crumpled it up, and threw it at him. "There," I said. "There's your dollar."

He stood up, picked up the dollar, and walked over to the service elevator that ran directly up to ON24's offices. He pushed the Up button, then turned to me. "You are going to pay for this," he said. The doors opened. He stepped inside and was gone.

I learned later that Duc walked out of the elevator, face bleeding and swollen, asked where the CEO's office was, and walked into it.

"Sam Polk did this to me. I want him fired," he said. I can only imagine what Sharat's face looked like as he pushed his glasses up on his nose.

CHAPTER 12

Sex in the City

❑

I was fired, of course. I was devastated. What hurt the
most was that Sharat hadn't stood up for me. I knew it
was ridiculous, but I'd fantasized about him calling me from
his cell phone, telling me not to worry, that he'd take care of
everything. The ache in my heart was so intense that I'd go
into my bedroom and turn the stereo all the way up, so loud
that I disappeared into the music. But eventually the song
would end, and I'd be back in the crushing reality of my life.

What I wanted more than anything was to call Ben, to be
comforted by my twin, whom I missed every single day. But
I couldn't—he still refused to talk to me.

I called Columbia, to see if by some miracle I could come
back for the semester that began in two weeks. They had a
space for me. Once again, I fled across the country.

I just wanted to get my life back on track, make it through
college. I'd planned to major in economics, but I declared an
English major, figuring that since I'd always been a reader,
that gave me the best chance of graduating. I swore off drugs,
off fighting, off crime. I promised myself I'd stop getting in
trouble.

As soon as I arrived in New York, I went to my favorite
bar, The West End. I'd planned to return a conquering hero.

Instead, I returned in ignominy. I walked through the front door directly to the bar and ordered a Rolling Rock. I looked around to see if there was anyone I knew. No one. No free tables, either. Standing alone, I felt a rush of embarrassment. I walked into the other room. A few tables stopped their conversation to look at me and then turned back toward each other.

I was about to walk back to the bar when I heard a shriek. It came from a table in the back, a table full of girls. They were all staring at me. Sloane Taylor leapt to her feet, ran toward me, and launched herself into my arms.

"Sam Polk," she practically screamed. "What are you doing here?"

I looked around the room. Everyone was staring at me. I smiled, stood up taller.

"Surprise," I said. "I'm back."

Sloane told me she had to return to her table—it was a team dinner—but that I should call her. While everyone watched, I punched her number into my phone.

I invited Sloane over to study at my place, a room I'd rented on the sixth floor of a frat house. I was in such a state of disbelief that she might be interested in me that it wasn't until several hours later when Sloane was squeezing by me—the room was tiny—that I made a move. I pulled her into my lap and kissed her. She pulled back, laughed, and said, "Whoa, tiger." Then she leaned in to kiss me again.

When she agreed to stay for the night, I felt like I'd won the lottery. The next morning we both woke up with hacking coughs: bronchitis. We spent the next few days holed up in my room, with Sloane regularly lighting cigarettes, then looking at me and saying, "What? Am I a quitter?" Her eyes would slit and her whole body would shake when she laughed.

Sloane was everything I'd ever wanted in a woman. She wasn't just hot. She was *popular*. She'd been arguably the most popular girl at her elite Los Angeles private school, one that sends multiple kids a year to each Ivy League school. When I'd tell other kids from her school that I was dating Sloane Taylor, their eyes would widen. Other women would come up to me and say, "Your girlfriend is breathtaking."

But Sloane was no cheerleader. She was a killer, captain of her state championship tennis team in high school, and a starter for Columbia. She got straight As. When I first heard her Valley girl talk, peppered with *like* and *dude*, I thought I was smarter than her. Soon she was editing my papers.

There was one thing about Sloane that gave me pause. She was taking a few months off drinking and drugs at the suggestion of her spiritual counselor. I'd never met anyone with a spiritual counselor before. She called hers Linda. They spoke on the phone every week. Sloane said that they were dealing with some particularly tough issues, and that Linda had recommended she stop drinking and drugs for the duration. Sloane said she didn't mind if I drank or smoked the occasional joint, so I didn't mind that she didn't.

I began to understand why Sloane liked me when she introduced me to her father. She invited me to stay with her parents in Los Angeles over Christmas break. She picked me up from the airport and drove me to their stately two-story house in Bel-Air, an affluent neighborhood on the west side of LA.

The house was empty when we arrived. Soon her dad returned from golfing at one of the two country clubs he belonged to. Jack was a short, barrel-chested man with silver hair. Within a minute of our first conversation, he mentioned that he'd gone to Dartmouth undergrad and Stanford Law School, shook my hand harder than he needed to, and cut his daughter off midsentence.

Jack dominated that house. He spoke to his wife like she was an employee. At the dinner table, he'd lead conversations about current events but was interested only in his own opinions. If you disagreed with him, he became dismissive. He talked about all the books he'd recently read, declaring each one "good" or "bad."

That's how it was in my house, too. Our family revolved around Dad, who considered himself an intellectual, and spoke like he and Thomas Friedman were close friends ("Tommy").

I'd been thinking a lot about my dad. A month before, my mother reported that she'd received a phone call from a woman named Sherri. Sherri told my mom that she'd been having an affair with my dad for ten years. The reason she was calling was that my dad had just broken it off with her in order to pursue a new relationship with a younger woman. Sherri thought my mom deserved to know.

Within a day my family had been demolished like a condemned building. Daniel and Julia, thirteen and eleven, were yanked out of school and shipped off to North Carolina for two weeks to stay with relatives. Dad moved out, into an apartment. I wasn't particularly surprised, or even that upset by the news, but I had no interest in going home for the holidays. That's why Sloane invited me out to spend Christmas in LA with her parents—she didn't want me to spend the holidays alone.

Sloane seemed desperate to impress her father, even though he treated her with the same understated contempt with which he treated his wife. But he *was* impressed by Sloane. He talked constantly about her accomplishments. Also, she was the only one in the family who'd go toe-to-toe with him during arguments, and he obviously loved that about her.

Sometimes he expressed his love physically, especially when he was drunk. He was always grabbing her, or pulling her into hugs. Sometimes she struggled to break free.

I disliked Jack Taylor for how he touched and spoke to his daughter, but I also admired his accomplishments: Ivy League schools, power job, money. He was a member of two country clubs. He drove an antique Mercedes; his wife drove a brand-new SUV. Their house was expensive but understated. The carpeting and furniture were all made of soft fabrics in different patterns that somehow seemed to match. Their weekly family restaurant had a sommelier.

But it was the small things I really loved. The *New York Times*, *Los Angeles Times*, and *Wall Street Journal* were delivered to their porch each day. Their liquor cabinet was stocked with brand-name labels—Ketel One, Grey Goose. Their Sub-Zero refrigerator kept vegetables restaurant crisp. They had DVDs of movies currently in theaters. Even their Chinese takeout was somehow better. And Jack wore pressed khakis and Ralph Lauren sweaters . . . on a *Saturday*.

It was during this visit that I began to understand that Jack Taylor's life is what graduating from Columbia made possible. He was a management consultant at McKinsey. McKinsey recruited on Columbia's campus. So did Goldman Sachs, J.P. Morgan, and Bain. If I could get my foot in the door at one of these firms, I could have a life like Jack Taylor's, the life my dad always wanted, instead of the life I grew up with—rented houses, junky cars, paycheck to paycheck.

Halfway through my visit to the Taylors', Sloane and I went out for a run, and I accidentally tracked dog shit up the stairs and into the bedroom. We didn't discover it until her mother knocked at the bedroom; she had followed the tracks from the front door. She insisted it wasn't a big deal and refused to let me clean it up. I saw her an hour later, sitting on the stairs, scrubbing the carpet with a brush.

I was so mortified I felt nauseous. I couldn't even *walk* through a nice home without ruining it, let alone live in one. I imagined Sloane's parents whispering about me in the privacy of their bedroom, shaking their heads.

As Sloane and I got closer and closer, I started to show a side of myself that I'd never exposed before. On Valentine's Day, I woke up at 4:00 a.m. to go all the way to the end of

Manhattan to buy two dozen red roses from the flower market, then sat outside for three hours in the February snow to get free tickets to a Broadway show, and on the way home stopped to buy live lobsters from a fish store. When Sloane came home that night, I'd covered her apartment in roses and candles.

I felt something that I'd never felt before, which was that I was no longer the absolute center of my world. Now Sloane was.

I told her I loved her; she told me she loved me back.

But it wasn't all roses and Broadway shows. She was bossy and got frustrated with me easily. She wasn't afraid to tell me what was wrong with my clothes. The harder she was on me, the more desperately I craved her. The more I pursued, the more she pushed me away. Our most frequent struggle was around sex.

I craved sex. I wanted it more often, in more varied styles. She wanted it less often, in less varied styles. I wanted her to do things that made her uncomfortable. So we fought. When I got drunk, I angrily demanded it.

She didn't understand how important sex was to me. Sex was the most validating thing I knew. I'd been desperate for sex since puberty but largely unsuccessful in getting it, at least from the women I wanted it from.

But in a relationship it was supposed to be different— easily accessible and frequent. After two or three days of not having sex, my resentment started to build. I'd feel angry that I wasn't being taken care of. Each day that resentment would grow bigger and bigger. If we hadn't had sex in a week and one of my friends made a comment about how hot Sloane was, instead of feeling pride I'd feel shame. Then anger. At her.

When we did have sex, I'd feel relief, especially if I lasted more than a few minutes. I'd be kind and sweet to Sloane, while inside I'd be patting myself on the back. *Yeah, baby.*

Well done. Then a day or two would pass, and the resentment would start to build again.

What began as a skirmish became a full-fledged battle when Sloane and I decided to spend the summer in Los Angeles. We rented an apartment together right off the Sunset Strip, a small one bedroom with a balcony in a *Melrose Place–*style complex.

I got a job at a small Internet company and spent my free time on the couch smoking weed, drinking coffee, and watching old movies from Blockbuster; or, if Sloane wasn't home, looking at porn on the computer. When Sloane was home, we fought. The same thing happened over and over again. Sloane and I started kissing on the couch. I moved to take her clothes off. She pulled away.

"What's wrong?" I asked.

"Nothing," she said, and we started again. I could tell she wasn't into it. But I pressed on, firmly, until she said, "Stop. I can't do this right now."

I tried to be nice, but inside I was furious. I turned on the TV and didn't look at her. She snuggled up close to me. I put my arm around her but wouldn't look at her. Finally, she asked, "Are you mad?" and I said, "Not at all." But I was.

Somehow I had to punish her for not sleeping with me, for *making me feel this way.* I tried again, later, when we were in bed for the night.

"Sam," she said, "I don't feel like it."

I knew I wasn't being the guy I wanted to be. I was drinking too much and smoking lots of weed. I was aware that what I was doing in the bedroom was inconsistent with being in love. But I couldn't stop pushing Sloane for sex. I needed the feeling that came after I fucked her. I needed it to fill the void.

After months of this, she said *enough* and insisted I go with her to see her counselor, Linda Redford, for couples counseling.

CHAPTER 13

Spiritual Counselor

◻

Linda was around fifty, with a gangly California look. She was six feet tall and had long blond hair. When we walked into her office, she enveloped Sloane in a hug. Then she looked at me, and I knew she wanted to hug me, too. I turned away and sat down on the white couch. Sloane sat next to me. Linda sat in a soft armchair facing us.

"So," she said, putting her hands on her knees, "first I want to thank you for coming, Sam. That took courage."

I told her I had a few questions. "Where did you get your PhD?" I asked, already knowing the answer.

"I don't have a PhD," Linda said. "Or a masters. I completed a three-year program in psychosynthesis, and I have a Certificate of Ordainment from the Association for the Integration of the Whole Person," she said.

I almost laughed out loud. *Um, the Association of what?* She hadn't even gone through an accredited program.

"Well," I said, shooting Sloane a look, "then how is it that you are a therapist?"

Sloane glared at me.

Linda smiled.

"I am not a therapist. I am a spiritual counselor. I'm a

Cherokee by descent, and my teachings are based in Native American philosophy and traditions."

I'm pretty sure insurance is not going to cover this.

"My practice runs on word of mouth," continued Linda. "People find me when they need me. I help make them whole again."

I didn't understand what she meant by making people whole, and I didn't really care about Native American philosophy. I was about to say something to this effect, when I remembered the chill in the air between Sloane and me at breakfast that morning. We hadn't had sex for weeks. We'd fought the night before because she wanted to watch *Felicity* and I wanted to watch *Law & Order*. We were dropping into longer and longer silences.

I saw Linda watching me.

"Do you have any more questions, Sam?" she asked.

"No," I said. "I'm good. We can start."

"Good. Sam, since it's your first time, why don't you begin? You can talk about whatever is going on with you."

"Just talk about anything?" I asked.

"Yes," Linda said. "I'd like to learn a little about where you are."

I laughed, exasperated.

"Um, okay," I said. "Sam in a few words. I don't have many friends. I'm at couples therapy with my girlfriend, with whom I fight all the time. Mostly, I'm alone. Other than that, things are great."

When she didn't respond and just kept looking at me with a warm smile, I realized I'd been waiting for a rebuke. She nodded, as if to encourage me. To fill the silence, I started talking again.

I talked about the fights Sloane and I were getting into, how insecure I was when we accompanied her parents for cocktails at their friends' mansions, me wearing my only nice sweater, which had a hole in it. I talked about my family, how my twin brother hadn't spoken to me for four years, and the recent revelation of my father's long-term affair.

"How did you feel when you learned of the affair?" Linda asked.

Growing up in LA you learn what earthquakes feel like. Mostly, they're not like they are in movies—walls don't crumble, massive fissures don't appear in the ground. Instead, you feel a powerful but distant rumbling. A deep vibration that is not violent in itself but in what it reveals—which is that solid ground, the very foundation upon which we build our lives, is not so solid after all. Earthquakes aren't scary because the ground shakes a lot; they're scary because the ground shakes at all. Learning about my dad's affair felt like an earthquake—distant, but powerful.

Linda motioned for me to continue. While I talked, I kept my eyes down. Sometimes I'd lift them to find Linda looking at me, her eyes kind. She'd nod encouragingly. She'd chuckle when I said something funny.

I talked and talked and talked. Words poured out unprompted, like they'd been bottled and shaken. We had two hours scheduled, and I'd been sure we wouldn't be able to fill all that time. When I glanced at the clock, I saw that an hour and a half had passed. I realized with horror how long I'd been talking, and clamped my mouth shut.

Linda smiled.

"I'm so glad you felt safe enough to share that with us, Sam. I'm sure Sloane is as well." I looked at Sloane, who smiled at me. I was mortified.

"Now, there is something Sloane would like to discuss," Linda said. "Okay if we change subjects?"

I was exhausted. I nodded.

"Would you feel comfortable," Linda asked me, "sharing a little about what the issues around sex have been like for you and Sloane?"

Um, no.

"Well, here's an example," I said. "When I came to LA over Christmas, Sloane picked me up at the airport. When we got to her house, no one was home. We went upstairs to her room. We hadn't seen each other in three weeks. And I wanted to have sex. I mean, it had been a long time!"

Linda nodded.

"We start kissing, but after a minute Sloane pulls away and gets out of bed and starts organizing her drawers. I'm like, *What the fuck?* in my mind. If there is any time, now should be it, but she doesn't want to. It sucked."

I'd worked myself into a huff. I glared at Sloane.

Linda said that sounded really hard for me.

Then Linda turned to Sloane. "What did it feel like to hear Sam say that?" Sloane looked like she was going to cry.

"It's true," Sloane said. "I feel so terrible about it. I want to have sex. I want to want to have sex. But sometimes I can't. Sometimes I just shut down." She turned to look directly at me. "I'm really sorry that it's so hard for you. It's hard for me, too. I feel like something is wrong with me."

I must have looked incredulous, because she sort of pulled back. But I wasn't angry; I was shocked. I'd assumed she didn't like sex sort of how I don't like Brussels sprouts. I hadn't imagined that she was upset about it, too. For a moment I understood what a bully I'd been.

Linda asked Sloane if she wanted to share with me some of the things that were going on with her. Sloane nodded and she pulled her knees up to her chest with her feet under her. She looked like a little girl. She said she was working through some stuff with her dad. While she was working on this stuff, she said, being sexual felt uncomfortable.

"Do you understand, Sam?" asked Linda.

"Not really," I said.

"Let me explain a few things," Linda said. "Sloane's father

has some trouble seeing how his actions impact his children. Sloane is dealing with some boundary violations that have had a significant impact on her."

My body was tense. I knew I'd done some boundary violating of my own.

"I'm not her dad," I said.

"That's true, Sam. And it's Sloane's responsibility to not put her feelings toward him on you. Sometimes she struggles with that. Like everything, it's a process. But there *are* certain similarities between you and her father. That is one of the reasons you two are together. Sometimes, if we have a wound inside us that we need to heal, we seek out situations or partners with whom we can re-create that historical dynamic. That's one of the reasons Sloane was attracted to you, and the same likely holds true for you."

Parents, parents, parents. I'm an adult, and this is bullshit.

I checked my watch—only fifteen minutes to go.

CHAPTER 14

Like Father, Like Son

◻

Six months later, Sloane left to study abroad in Florence. I was glad. I'd had my eyes on two girls whose glances had lingered on mine in the library, and by the time Sloane called from Florence two weeks into the semester, I'd slept with both of them. Sloane was in tears—she said she'd made a mistake going to Italy. She asked if I would come visit her. I smiled as I felt the power shift to my side. I coolly told her time apart would be good for us.

This was perfect. When Sloane came back, we'd get back together. In the meantime, my focus would be on getting a high-caliber summer internship, so I could start building toward a life like Jack Taylor's.

In the spring, companies descend on Columbia's campus, recruiting for summer internships. There were several types of internships available—consulting, investment banking— but I'd known I wanted to work on a trading floor since I'd read *Liar's Poker* by Michael Lewis the year before. As he unveiled life on a trading floor—the card games during the workday, huge platters of onion cheeseburgers arriving at 10:00 a.m., the freedom to scream into your phone and slam it dramatically into the cradle—I thought, *People actually get paid for this?* They did. A lot. I was sold.

I'd applied to the trading department at every investment bank, but my sub-3.0 GPA made me an unlikely candidate. In the end I only got interviews at CSFB and Goldman Sachs. For Goldman, the GPA was ultimately a deal breaker. But CSFB was impressed with my entrepreneurial experience, and they invited me to the final vetting process known as Super Day.

That morning I took the subway from Columbia to CSFB's downtown headquarters for five back-to-back interviews. I was given a sticker with my name and college printed on it and led to the waiting area, where my fellow interviewees from schools like Harvard, Stanford, and the University of Chicago huddled nervously around the silver coffee dispensers and fresh fruit. Every few minutes the pretty young women of the human resources department came in, scanned the name-tagged students, and led the next interviewee away.

My first four interviews were mixed: some of the traders were impressed by my work experience, others by my stint as a Division I wrestler; all of them were concerned about my GPA. My final interviewer, a director named Taylor Madsen, was a former football star at Yale. As he walked in, I noted the caramel tan of a two-round-a-week golfer. From the non-chalance with which he held his finger up, cutting me off midsentence to take a call from his wife, I knew that *this* was the guy I needed to impress.

When he got off the phone, he scanned my resume. My stomach dropped. In addition to abysmal grades, my resume was littered with half-truths and obfuscations. I'd left out the fact I'd been suspended from Columbia and fired from ON24.

Taylor Madsen looked up from my resume and smiled.

"This work experience is amazing," he said. "And your timing is incredible. You left San Francisco a month before the dot-com boom ended!"

I nodded, terrified. My resume: a house of cards.

"Your grades suck," he continued, "but you're a wrestler so I know you're driven."

He paused.

"I like you," he said. "I'm going to get you this job."

I hadn't said a word. I started to thank him. He held his finger up, freezing me midsentence again, put his phone to his ear, and walked out of the room.

Years later I'd think back to that moment—how despite my poor grades and the lies on my resume, I'd gotten one of the most competitive internships in the world without speaking a word. It was as if the universe knew that I needed to go to Wall Street, needed to glimpse, like Dorothy in *The Wizard of Oz*, what was really behind the curtain.

The next few months were spectacular. With a summer internship in my back pocket, I spent most of my time at bars, chasing girls, drinking, and occasionally dabbling in drugs.

I started to dream about Sloane. She'd walk toward me, a glint in her eye, a pouty smile on her lips. She'd wrap her arms around my neck and kiss me softly. If I half woke up, I'd try to go back to sleep to get back in the dream. She was the first thing I thought about in the morning and the last thing I thought about at night. I thought about her when I was with other women.

I knew the minute her plane was scheduled to land, but I didn't call her. I was unwilling to sacrifice the hand I'd gained. *Better to let her call me*, I thought. She did. We agreed to meet for lunch.

Both of us were reserved, cautious, but soon conversation rippled between us. I told her excitedly about my internship, which started in two weeks. She told me she'd missed me. I paid the bill, and as we left the restaurant I casually asked her if she wanted to spend the evening together. I saw the relief flood her, and I pulled her to me and kissed her.

Later she came home with me, to the same place where

I'd slept with a girl named Cassandra the night before. That night, before Sloane and I had sex, I put on a condom because I'd been having unprotected sex with other women. It was the first time we'd used a condom since Sloane went on birth control. I saw her notice, and I thought she was going to say something, but she didn't.

Over the next few weeks I saw a lot of Sloane but continued to see the other women as well. I could tell by how Sloane avoided asking me about evenings I spent away from her that she knew.

CHAPTER 15

Brand-Name Life

◻

In June 2002, at the age of twenty-two, I stepped out of an elevator onto the CSFB trading floor on the first day of my summer internship.

The room was the size of an airplane hangar. Glass-walled offices fenced the perimeter. Rows and rows of trading desks stretched across the room. On the walls hung a hundred glowing flat-screen TVs. Each trader sat in front of six high-tech computer monitors and a phone turret with enough dials, knobs, and buttons to make it seem like a cockpit. My eyes fastened on a trader in a light-blue button-down. He was talking rapidly into the microphone tip of a headset. He looked like he was running the command center of a spaceship.

"That's Greco," said the HR woman who'd come up behind me, pointing at the trader I was staring at. "He trades telecom— Verizon, AT&T—on the corporate bond desk." Trading floors are laid out like school cafeterias—instead of each table belonging to a clique, each belonged to a certain market.

"You'll be on corporates for a month," said the HR woman, holding a clipboard, wearing pearls and a gray pantsuit. "Then you'll rotate to mortgages. It'll be between you and two other interns; only one of you will be offered a full-time job. Good luck."

Getting that offer was the whole point of my summer. I was approaching the elbow between college and the real world, where an Ivy League education was most concretely valuable, where securing a full-time position at a prestigious firm meant entrance into the highest echelon of American capitalism. The first step toward becoming one of the business leaders you read about in the paper.

When markets were up, banks hired every one of their interns. But now that the Internet bubble had burst, and the stock market's value had declined by half, turning an internship into a full-time job had grown difficult. I was terrified about not securing a position at a blue-chip firm and disappearing into the anonymity of regular life.

I watched as the HR woman walked back to her office, passing rows of men glued to their computer screens. One trader strolled down the aisle casually swinging a golf club. Some were on the phone and I could hear the hum of conversation like in a restaurant. The atmosphere was focused, professional—nothing like the shouting and waving of the trading floors on TV.

I realized I was gawking. I didn't have any idea what to do, or where to stand. My face flushed. I saw Anna, a junior trader who'd interviewed me. She looked up, a phone pressed to her ear. I waved. She smiled. Then her eyes flicked back to her screens.

I walked over and stood behind her chair. I figured she'd sense my presence and get off the phone and I could ask her what I should be doing. I didn't realize at the time that standard rules of propriety don't apply on a Wall Street trading floor. In the weeks ahead I'd become accustomed to standing behind a trader for fifteen, twenty minutes before they'd even acknowledge me.

After a minute I thought maybe she hadn't seen me so I stepped closer. She didn't even look up; she just speared an index finger into the air, indicating that I should wait. I felt conspicuous, embarrassed. I stood there for ten minutes before Anna hung up the phone. "Grab a folding chair from that closet," she said.

My job was to learn how a trading floor worked by watching and asking questions. But the last thing in the world a trader wanted was some college kid peppering her with questions, so in reality my job was to fade into the background, like furniture. I spent the morning listening to Anna and scribbling notes to appear busy. By early afternoon, unaccustomed to adult workdays, I was struggling to keep my eyes open when a trader across the aisle stood up holding a World War II infantry helmet. "It's time," he said.

Everyone laughed and reached for their wallets. "That's Jared Caldwell," Anna said. "He trades energy. He's a stud." The next few minutes consisted of traders flicking their gold and silver credit cards into Jared's helmet. When all the cards had been collected, Jared picked a card, read out the name, and then tossed the card back to the person it belonged to. Then again and again and again, while traders ribbed one another, chortling when their own names were called. When just two cards were left, everyone knew whose they were. Jared picked one out and put it facedown on the desk. Then he grabbed the last card.

"Today," Jared said, "coffee is on . . . Hinton!" The group exploded, laughing and yelling. "Where's the intern?" Jared yelled. I hustled over. He shook my hand, gave me Hinton's credit card, and told me to go to Dunkin' Donuts and get coffee for the whole desk. I walked toward the elevators with a huge smile across my face. This was fun!

That night I went out with the other interns. A willowy French girl from Georgetown laughed loudly when I told the group how I'd stood behind a trader for twenty minutes without being acknowledged. She kept glancing at me, and when she went to the bar for a drink, I followed. Her name was Melanie, and soon we were chatting, just the two of us. Two managing directors showed up; they both leered at Melanie as they talked.

Two hours later, I was drunk. When Melanie said she was leaving, I said I was, too, and soon we were pressed against a building making out. I asked Melanie to come home with me, to the Alphabet City apartment I was subletting with another finance guy. She said no, that she had to wake up early.

Reluctantly, I stumbled home alone. I packed some pot into a glass pipe I kept in the drawer next to my bed, smoked, and went to sleep.

I was on the trading floor by five thirty the next morning. I asked Jared, the trader with the credit card helmet, if I could sit with him. "Sure," he said. "Just plug in this headset, and you can listen to all my calls. Write down any questions, and I'll answer them at the end of the day."

I spent the rest of the morning listening to Jared's calls, safely blending into the background. In the afternoon, Jared spent twenty minutes answering my questions, mostly about what certain words meant in the foreign language of trader-speak.

"Anything else?" he asked after answering my last question.

"Yeah," I said. "Who is that?" I pointed to the biggest office on the floor, where a tall good-looking blond man in his thirties sat reclined in his chair, his feet propped on the desk. I'd seen him walking the floor earlier. People had stood to shake his hand.

"That's Jack DiMaio," Jared said. "He's thirty-five and the boss of the whole floor." Jared told me how Jack had organized a walkout when the traders thought they were being underpaid; to entice them to return, management had given all the traders three-year multi-million-dollar bonus guarantees. Jack was guaranteed $15 million per year and named head of fixed income.

I looked at Jack, reclined in his office, and bristled with envy. I imagined myself in his position, my feet propped on the desk. The boss of the whole floor.

The next day I was sitting with Jared again when Jack DiMaio called him. I looked to Jared to see if he wanted privacy, but he motioned for me to listen. After a few minutes of talking about the market, the conversation turned casual. Jared, a car aficionado, said he admired Jack's new Porsche. "Well," said Jack, "then as a part of this year's bonus, it's yours."

I almost fainted. I'd dreamt of being rich since I was a kid. But I'd never imagined a world where people gave each other $70,000 cars in a casual phone call.

Before that summer, the most successful guy I knew was Sloane's father. At CSFB, I saw a thousand Jack Taylors, men who had gone to brand-name schools and gotten jobs in brand-name firms and wore brand-name clothes in their brand-name lives. They lived in places like Darien and Greenwich, took Caribbean vacations, and belonged to country clubs. The most important thing in my life was getting what they had.

I spent the next few weeks working feverishly. I was the first one on the desk in the morning, arriving at 5:00 a.m. At night there were dinners and drinks with traders and executives, and how well you performed in those situations was as critical as your performance on the desk. Getting a full-time job offer was not based on how smart you were. It was a question of whether the traders liked you.

They wanted to know if I was cool. Did I play a sport in college? Which one? There is a hierarchy of athletics on Wall Street: Lacrosse at the top, crew at the bottom. Wrestling was right in the middle—not as cool as soccer or basketball, but tough enough to impress.

They also wanted to know how social you were. Time after time veterans told me that Wall Street works hard, but they play harder. You had to prove that you could handle yourself in a bar.

To the traders, as an intern, I was an afterthought. To me, they were the most important people in the world. I can rattle off the names of those CSFB corporate bond traders like I can the seventh-grade cheerleaders from junior high. They were the gatekeepers of my future.

I went out every night. I rarely called Sloane, and when she called me I often didn't answer. One night, I hooked up with two girls in the same night. The first was a Duke sorority girl I'd met on Super Day, and when she left my apartment I was still drunk and still looking to party. So I called an engineering major at Columbia whom I'd hooked up with often while Sloane was in Italy and invited her over. By the time she arrived I was nearly blacked out. We started to have sex. I pushed her to do things she didn't like. She got pissed, stormed home. I passed out.

CHAPTER 16

The Fulcrum

◘

Four weeks into my internship, Jared and I had become close, some of the traders—Greco, Jory, Hinton—seemed to like me, and I'd received several compliments on my work ethic. Sloane had gotten a waitressing job at the trendy Soho House and was taking a summer class at NYU. That Friday, after work, I was so exhausted that I went home and climbed straight into bed. I spent all of Saturday on my couch, watching TV and smoking weed.

The next day, Sunday, July 22, 2002, my high school friend Nate Robertson was in town, and he invited me to play in a softball game in Central Park. I hadn't worked out once that summer, was about thirty pounds overweight, and was afraid I'd look stupid. In my first at bat, I nearly struck out before hitting a lazy pop-up to left-center, straight into the outfielder's glove. But in the last inning, as I was playing shortstop, the batter hit a high-bouncing ground ball far to my left, and I made a blind underhanded stab at it—a prayer, really, that was answered as the ball sailed cleanly into the pocket of my glove. I ripped it out and flung a dart to first. Over the next few weeks I'd think often about the easy happiness of that moment.

After the game we smoked a joint and walked over to The

West End, that bar I'd frequented at Columbia, for wings and pitchers. At the bar, I received a text from Sloane saying she needed to talk to me. I was stoned but knew immediately that something was wrong. I called her, but when she heard I was at a bar she said we'd talk later, when I was no longer drunk and high. I left the bar immediately and started walking to the subway, my stomach in knots.

I jumped in a cab instead of taking the subway. I wanted to get to my Alphabet City sublet fast, call her up, and tell her I was sorry. Make things right. I'd do whatever she wanted. I'd stop seeing other women. I'd slow down on the drinking and the pot. I'd apologize. Whatever it took to win her back.

By the time I arrived home, it was dark outside. I called Sloane. Half an hour later she walked through the front door. Her face was pale, serious.

"There's something I need to say to you," I said.

"Me first," she said.

The sublet was two stories—the first floor and the basement. Sloane and I went downstairs to my bedroom, a cave with no windows, and sat on the bed facing each other. I tried to show her with my eyes that I loved her.

"I love you, Sam, but I don't want to be with you anymore."

I felt like I'd been struck by a speeding car. I started to argue with her. She put her hand up, silencing me.

"I'm sorry, Sam," she said. "I don't like who you've become."

I was hit with a rush of pain so fierce that I couldn't breathe. She left the room.

I needed to catch her. I jumped up, ran up the stairs, and flew out the front door and down the steps onto the street.

I saw a cab rolling toward the end of the block. She must have gotten in it. I ran after it, but it turned the corner.

She was gone.

I stood in the middle of the street, feeling like a hole had ripped open in my chest. After a minute, I went back inside and sat down on the couch. I'd expected an exchange, a push-pull. I'd expected ultimatums. But there was nothing incremental in her actions. She was done playing.

I made my way downstairs and lay in bed. I curled myself into a ball. It felt like my internal organs had exploded. My neck muscles felt like suspension cables.

A sack of weed sat on my bed. I retrieved a pipe and started to pack it. Halfway through, I stopped. I suspected that if I got drunk or high I might fall into a darker abyss, and I had no idea what would happen if I did. I put the weed back in the Ziploc bag and put it away. I lay down again.

After a time I went upstairs. The apartment was dark and quiet. I wrapped myself in a blanket and sat on the couch. Bruce Springsteen had released *The Rising* that summer, and I turned it up on the stereo.

I stayed up all night, sitting on the couch, smoking cigarettes, staring into nothing. By sunrise I was dizzy. The heartache throbbed. I had to be at work in a few hours, but that seemed impossible. The only thing that could make the pain stop was getting Sloane back. I walked over to the NYU building where she had rented a room. I took a seat on the curb and hunched forward with my arms wrapped around myself. A woman walking by asked if I was okay. I nodded, turned away.

I waited for over an hour. Finally Sloane came out, wearing a black dress for her waitressing job at Soho House. I stood up and yelled out her name. She looked shocked, then scared. I started toward her.

"No!" she shouted. A cab pulled up in front of her and she opened the door and then said, sharply, "Go to work, Sam." She got in the cab and it drove away. I stood there in the street, alone.

I walked home. It was seven. I was already late. I put on

my clothes without showering or shaving and took a cab to work. Soon the elevator doors were opening and I was walking onto the trading floor. I sat down somewhere and tried to look busy for about an hour. Then I looked at my watch. Only ten minutes had passed. I wasn't going to make it.

I couldn't do anything but be honest. I went up to Anna, the junior trader whom I had shadowed on my first day. I told her my girlfriend had broken up with me, and I was in too much pain to be at work. Despite her hardened demeanor on the floor, Anna was compassionate that day. Maybe she herself was a veteran of difficult relationships. In an act of kindness I've remembered ever since, she said she would cover for me. She'd tell the other traders I was at an intern event all day. I thanked her and left.

When I got home, I returned to my cocoon on the couch. The air was quiet. A shaft of sunlight speared the room and I saw dust particles floating in it. I lit a cigarette.

I don't like who you've become, Sloane had said. Those words were a knife in my heart, but at the same time they held a mirror to it. She didn't like who I'd become. Neither, I realized, did I.

I was tired. Tired of lying. Tired of hurting other people. Tired of ruining everything that was important to me. Tired of numbing. Mostly, I was tired of myself. I wanted to be a different person. I wanted to live a different kind of life.

CHAPTER 17

Remnants of an Accident

◻

"Do you know why Sloane broke up with you?" Linda asked. I'd called her and asked for help.

"Not exactly," I said carefully.

"Why don't you tell me what's happened since the last time we spoke?"

I was accustomed to guarding my secrets, but now I shared everything. About the other girls, about the drugs and drinking, about how I'd treated Sloane when she was in Italy, about how I'd treated her since she got back.

When I was finished, Linda was quiet.

"Sam," she finally said, "what do you want?"

"To get Sloane back," I said.

"It doesn't sound like that's possible," she said.

"Well, then," I said, "I want the pain to stop."

"I'm not sure that's possible, either," she said. "At least not for a while. You've been suppressing feelings for a long time. It'll get harder before it's easier."

She asked if I would stop drinking and using drugs. When I told her I had a bag of weed downstairs, she suggested I dump it in the toilet with her on the phone. When I opened the bag, the pungent smell of marijuana slapped me. I held the buds in my hand for a second and then dropped them into the toilet. Watching them swirl down the drain was one of the scariest things I'd ever seen. I was unarmored.

She asked if I was willing to go to an AA meeting. I told her I'd go.

She asked me to commit to doing the following things daily: shower, work out, eat healthy, and write in a journal. "These will help you start feeling good about yourself," she said. She also asked that I go back to work.

"There's one more thing," she said before we got off the phone. "I'd like you to start working on a letter of apology to Sloane. You need to make amends."

A letter will get her to come back, I heard.

I'd been using pot, alcohol, NyQuil, or Valium to fall asleep for years; that night, despite the fact that I hadn't slept a wink the night before, I tossed and turned for hours. I'd only just fallen asleep when my alarm went off at 4:30 a.m. I staggered out of bed. There was a gym in the basement of CSFB, and when I stood in front of the mirror in the locker room I grabbed handfuls of fat on my stomach and silently screamed at myself. I made it just ten minutes on the StairMaster before I was gasping for air and had to stop.

I took the elevator to the trading floor. Jared called me over and started asking where I'd been the day before. I felt like if I spoke I'd burst into tears, so I put my finger up and went into the bathroom. When I came out, I ignored Jared, found an empty desk. I tried to read economic reports to appear busy, but it was as if I were reading Arabic. It felt like the day had been extended from ten hours to forty million. Every hour, I walked to the bathroom, went into a stall, sat on the toilet, put my head in my hands, and allowed myself five minutes of peace.

On my walk home, I staggered down the street like a refugee, stopping to lean against buildings for support. Once I bent at the waist, thinking I was going to throw up. I poured sweat.

When I got home, I started to work on the letter to Sloane. I described in detail how much pain I was in without her. I begged her to come back.

That night I called Linda and read it to her.

"You are going to need to rewrite this," she said.

I needed to take out any mention of Sloane's part in the situation, Linda said, as well as any requests for her to come back. "Look for your part," she suggested.

Fuck this, I thought. *That's not going to help me get her back.* But I also knew the letter as I had written it wasn't going to, either. I'd seen Sloane's face on that street corner when she told me to go to work. She wasn't kidding.

After work the next day, I sat down to work again on the letter. I took out the begging, the blaming. I spent hours on it, taking responsibility, each sentence a struggle. When the letter was done, I knew Linda couldn't have any problem with it.

She didn't. She congratulated me on writing it. Then she told me to put it in a drawer. There might be a time I could send that letter to Sloane, but not now. Sloane had made it clear she needed space. Part of my amends would be honoring that.

Rage swelled inside me as I thought about all the time I'd wasted on the letter. Then the rage burst like a dam, and I put my head in my hands and cried. Sloane wasn't coming back.

When I ran out of tears, Linda told me to read the letter again, and this time to remember it was about *me*.

As I read out loud, I thought back to the steel in Sloane's face, and I understood how that had been forged. She was standing up for herself against a guy who said he loved her but treated her like garbage.

The next day at work I rotated from the corporate desk to the mortgage desk. Instead of trying to ingratiate myself with my new team, every hour I'd go down the elevator, walk to the park across the street, and smoke cigarettes and think about Sloane. When I came back to the trading floor, I scrubbed my hands and face with soap and rinsed my mouth out to erase the scent.

When I got home, I sat on the couch and dialed Ben's number. After the fifth ring, I was about to hang up. He picked up. "What do you want?" he said.

"I need help," I said, and burst into tears. I told him about Sloane. I told him I hadn't used drugs or alcohol since the breakup. I told him I'd barely eaten. I told him I was in trouble.

I took a breath. "Will you come down and stay with me?" I asked. It was a crazy request.

Ben paused. I heard in that pause an acknowledgment of five years' separation. Of all the things I'd messed up in my life, my relationship with my twin brother was by far the most painful. His silence meant that it'd been hard for him, too.

During the five years we hadn't spoken, I'd heard stories about Ben. He'd gotten in eleven fights his freshman year at Cornell. Some were legendary. One night, a starter on the Cornell hockey team, a bear of a man who would go on to play in the NHL, arrived at a party and picked a fight with Ben. It looked, I was told later, like David versus Goliath. People thought my brother would finally get what was coming to him. But it didn't go down that way. A group of men had to pull my brother off the hockey player's prone body after girls started screaming, "He's going to kill him."

After Ben graduated, he'd gone to Korea and Vietnam to teach English and drink. Now he was in upstate New York, working as a counselor at Paul Newman's camp for terminally ill kids.

"I'll take the train," he said.

CHAPTER 18

The Easy Confidence
of Millionaires

◻

When Ben arrived at my apartment, he sat next to me on the couch. With him next to me it was like my burden had been split in two. At the same time, what had happened five years before sat heavily between us. I knew it wasn't the time to discuss that, but there was something else I needed to bring up with Ben.

"There's something I have to ask you," I said. My heart hammered in my chest. Ben looked up at me.

"I need you to not drink while you are here."

I was terrified Ben would tell me to fuck off, and leave. But Linda had said that this "boundary" was of the utmost importance.

Ben looked at me for a long moment, then nodded.

When I rolled out of bed at 4:30 a.m. the next morning, I left Ben snoring on the couch and headed to the bank's gym, where I climbed on the StairMaster. Two rows ahead of me on the bikes were Brady Dougan, the head of the investment bank, and Matt Ruppel, the thirty-year-old head of mortgage trading, a former collegiate wrestling champ. Their bodies were tight and sinewy. They had the easy confidence of millionaires. While I pumped up and down on the StairMaster, I watched them talk and allowed myself the fantasy that one day I might be in their position.

That night I was the last one on the desk. I was packing my bag when Zach Stephens, the head of mortgage sales, walked by. He asked where I was headed.

"The intern event down the street," I responded. I'd planned to show my face for a few minutes and then slip out quietly so I could get back home.

"Me, too," Zach said. "We'll walk together."

A week ago I would have paid money to spend time alone with Zach, but now I would have paid not to. But he was a managing director; I couldn't say no.

Zach was tall and muscular with a long, rapid stride. I hustled to keep up. Fortunately, he was a comfortable talker, and I only had to supply a few questions about his start on Wall Street to keep him talking for most of the ten-block walk. Near the end, he suddenly accelerated into a higher gear and was ten feet ahead of me before I noticed. He passed a woman in a black dress and turned to stare at her, his head cocked diagonally so he could get the best view.

When I finally caught up to him, he said, "I had to get a good look at those tits."

I thought that's just how guys talked about women. But that day, for the first time, I heard the hostility in Zach's words. I remembered earlier that day when Zach's wife had called. He'd told his assistant to put her on hold and kept her there a full five minutes before he picked up.

Three days later, Saturday, I sat at an outdoor café with Ben in the early afternoon. He'd gone out the night before and gotten drunk. I'd heard him puking in the bathroom. We hadn't spoken about it. But his drinking lay between us like a gauntlet.

"So, what . . . are you never going to drink again?" Ben said.

"I can't think about it like that," I said. "I'm not even sure I'm going to make it till next week."

I paused.

"But I want to," I said.

"Why?" he asked.

"Remember how successful you and I were growing up? Spelling bees, Mock Trial, editor of the newspaper. Since we started drinking, I've been arrested, suspended from Columbia, and fired from a great job. And you?" I asked, knowing the answer.

In college Ben had been arrested twice. One time, he walked into the frat house of a guy who'd harassed his girlfriend, strode into the guy's bedroom, and slugged him in the face. To make ends meet during college, Ben had supported himself by writing papers for other students. He'd charge $20 per page and guarantee an A grade no matter what subject. But his own grades had been abysmal.

Ben nodded, as if satisfied with my answer. But I knew I'd held something back.

"It's more than that, though," I said, my throat full. "Here's the truth. I cheated on Sloane. Multiple times. I lied to her about it."

"It's college," Ben said. "Everyone does."

"I don't think that's true," I said. "And it's not just that. It's like I spend all this time trying to be this cool guy. But deep down, I don't like who I am. I want to be proud of myself. And I'm not."

Ben looked searchingly at me. We'd spent our whole lives pretending things were okay. Now we sat in the silence brought on by my admission that they were not.

A week later, my dad came to New York for a business trip. I hadn't talked to him since Sloane dumped me. I was afraid he wouldn't understand why I'd stopped drinking and smoking pot.

He called and asked if I would have dinner with him. I asked him not to drink while he was with me. He agreed.

When I walked up to the restaurant, he was sitting at a table on the sidewalk. There was a fresh Manhattan to the left of his water glass.

"Hey buddy," he said. "So good to see you."

He pulled me into a hug. I squirmed out and sat across from him.

"What a beautiful day," he said with contrived innocence.

"Dad . . ." I forced out. I was raw, fragile. I'd barely made it through the past two weeks. His disregard for my request felt like a punch in the stomach. It was always like this—my words went in his ears and disappeared, never to be thought about again.

"Dad," I started again. "What the hell?"

"Oh," he said, looking at his drink. "It's just one."

Then, seeing my contorted face, he picked it up, drained the glass, and put it down. *Problem solved*, his look said.

I pushed my chair back with a sharp grating peal and stood up. He looked up in surprise. I looked down at him with a mixture of fury and helplessness. I stood on the edge of collapse. For the first time in my life, I thought, *I deserve better*. Right now I needed to be around people who treated me gently. Dad had never been gentle.

I turned and walked away. I heard him shout after me, but I kept walking.

The last month of my CSFB internship was the longest month of my life. At work, I fantasized about the refuge of my couch. My performance on the mortgage sales desk was abysmal. I tried to seem interested and attentive, but my mind always drifted to Sloane. I'd sneak out three or four times a day to smoke cigarettes in the park.

While my performance was weak, there were small victories. I didn't miss another day of work. I worked out every single morning, ate salads instead of burgers. I talked to Linda or went to a meeting almost every day. Amidst the devastation of my life, I collected these small achievements. They felt important, somehow—the first green shoots after a nuclear winter. I was, for once, more focused on taking care of myself than on fitting in or impressing people.

But it was more than that. Over the past few years, every story I'd told about myself—Sam the wrestler, Sam the Columbia student, Sam the Internet entrepreneur—had been smashed. Now, stripped of the one person I loved, my Wall Street story falling apart, I began to understand that those narratives didn't define me. In a sense, during those weeks after Sloane dumped me, I met myself for the first time.

Every afternoon, I'd swing by the corporate desk to visit Jared Caldwell and the other corporate traders, to make sure they remembered me. I wanted so badly to be a part of that team.

Two weeks after Ben went back to Paul Newman's camp in upstate New York, he called me and told me he hadn't drank since he left. He said it was the hardest thing he'd ever done, but he was going to see if he could make it a month.

I saw Sloane one more time that summer. It was one of those breezy August days in Manhattan where you hear the tinkling hum of people eating and drinking outside and no matter how you are feeling you have to stop and thank whatever it is you believe in for the privilege of living in this majestic, bustling city. I came out of the subway in shirtsleeves. The wind dried the sweat on my back.

I didn't have any plans, but I didn't want to go straight home. Sloane's building was two blocks out of my way. I wasn't aiming to see her. I just wanted to be close, to stand outside her building and envision what she might be doing inside.

As I turned the corner, I saw her standing in the same place she'd stood the morning she told me to go to work. She was waiting for a cab, wearing the same black dress. I realized my presence might scare her, so I put my head down and continued walking. I was across the street and almost past her when I heard her call my name.

I looked up. She waved.

"Hi," I said, and continued on.

"Come over here," she called.

I stood a few feet from her, determined to give her all the space she needed. She reached across and hugged me. I held her gently for the most fleeting of moments. I didn't grasp as she pulled away.

"You've lost weight," she said.

I nodded. "Yes."

"How are you?" she asked.

I paused a second. "I'm okay, actually," I said. "How are you?"

"I've been better," she said.

Instead of feeling happy or wondering if she might be open to getting back with me, I just felt sad. "I'm sorry to hear that," I said.

We both stood there a moment.

"Well, I better be on my way," I said.

"Good-bye," she said. I nodded and turned away.

As I walked away I felt the heartbreak reemerge, but it was no longer as jagged. It'd somehow been softened by the knowledge that I'd handled myself like a man. A different kind of man than the one I had previously been, or even wanted to be.

On the last day of my internship I stood in an empty conference room, practicing the speech I'd prepared for Nasser, the head of corporate trading. I'd only spoken to him once that summer, to introduce myself. He was too high up to spend time with an intern. But I'd e-mailed him to ask if he'd grant me five minutes on my last day. It was a Hail Mary. He said yes.

I walked to his glass-walled office. He sat at his desk, staring at his trading screens. When I knocked, he held his finger in the air. I stood there, my palms sweaty and my stomach in knots.

He kept me waiting forty-five minutes. Finally, Jared walked up and asked what was going on. When I told him, he walked into Nasser's office, tapped him on the shoulder, and pointed to me. Nasser waved me in.

"Good luck, brother," said Jared as he walked out.

Nasser stood. I faced him across the desk.

"Nasser," I began, "first, I want to thank you for the opportunity—"

He held his hand up, cutting me off.

"Thank *you*, Sam. Thank you for your hard work. Whether you receive a full-time offer will not be my decision. The other traders will vote. I've been busy and obviously haven't gotten to spend much time with you, so it would be unfair of me to cast a deciding vote. Again, thank you for your work. If you'll excuse me, I have to get to a meeting."

I stood aside and watched the opportunity of a lifetime walk slowly away from me.

CHAPTER 19

Nurturing Love

◻

After my CSFB internship ended, I returned to Columbia for my final semester. A full five years had passed since I'd first arrived in New York as a Columbia freshman; it seemed bizarre that though so much had changed, I was still in the exact same place. I moved into a tiny dorm room with a loft bed and a desk underneath. To get onto the bed I had to step on the desk, brace my foot against the opposite wall, and launch myself up. The waking hours when I wasn't at the library I spent in my room fantasizing about being a trader on Wall Street, or reading *Drama of the Gifted Child* by Alice Miller, a book Linda suggested, about how childhood trauma manifests in adulthood.

A couple of weeks into the semester I got a call from CSFB saying I would not be offered a full-time position. I wasn't surprised, but I was devastated. I would graduate from Columbia in four months with a degree in English and no job. Approaching the end of college felt like sailing toward the edge of the world. Columbia was my badge of worth. I was afraid that after graduation, I'd disappear into the abyss of normalcy.

I started applying to other investment banks. Getting a job would be next to impossible. It was 2002. The Internet bubble had burst, WorldCom and Enron had imploded, and the economy was reeling. Wall Street wasn't hiring.

I called Taylor Madsen, the CSFB director who'd interviewed me at Super Day. He'd been assigned to me as a mentor and had remained supportive even after my performance began to decline.

"Do you know anyone who can help me?" I asked.

"I don't, Sam. I'm sorry."

Even though I hadn't gotten a full-time offer, I could tell he was still pulling for me. I took a last shot.

"What about Marshall Masters?" I asked.

Marshall Masters was a Wall Street legend. For years he'd been the biggest corporate bond trader in the market, known for making risky bets that always seemed to pay off. At Merrill Lynch, he'd been the youngest managing director in firm history. He'd run Merrill's trading desk for years and then gone to UBS, a second-tier trading shop, and led them to the number one ranking as the top corporate bond trading firm on The Street.

That summer, when I was at CSFB, headlines announced that Marshall Masters had left UBS for Bank of America in Charlotte. It was rumored that when Bank of America, then a third-tier trading shop, had asked the fifteen largest money managers in the market what head trader could take them to number one, all fifteen said Marshall Masters. Bank of America paid him a fortune.

Taylor thought for a moment. I knew Marshall and Taylor had started on Wall Street together, ten years earlier, and that they remained friends.

"You'd have to move to Charlotte," he said.

"I'll do anything," I said.

Taylor said he'd talk to Marshall, and he gave me Marshall's phone number.

I called Marshall Masters the next day, but he didn't pick

up. I was desperate for a job, so I called back the next day and left a message. He didn't call me back. I decided I was going to keep calling, every day, until I talked to him.

The last semester of my college career was looking bleak—no job, no Sloane. I signed up for a senior seminar class called Upward Mobility Stories in American Literature. There were only ten people in a seminar, and when I walked through the door, I saw Sloane seated at the table. I blushed and tried not to look at her.

When I told Linda that Sloane was in my seminar, she said it would be a good opportunity to practice.

"Practice what?" I asked.

"Nurturing love," she said.

I was getting used to how Linda talked, but that sounded corny even for her.

"Um, what?" I asked. She laughed.

She said that truly loving someone meant you care about what's best for them as much as yourself.

"Unfortunately," she said, "you didn't receive that kind of love growing up. So you are going to have to learn on your own."

I gave Sloane space. I smiled at her when I came into class but otherwise left her alone. She ignored me.

One day I returned to my room to find the light on my answering machine blinking. It was Marshall Masters. I'd called him every day for three weeks straight. I took a deep breath and dialed the number I now knew by heart.

"Hi Sam," he said when he picked up. "Thank you for being persistent. Taylor Madsen has never recommended someone, so I'm excited to meet you. I am going to have you come in and meet some people. We'll go from there. You'll have to go through the standard interview process, but I'm going to let HR know I'm interested."

I hung up the phone, hopeful for the first time in months.

Ben and I had started talking on the phone a couple of times a week. Our conversations were stilted and terse at first but soon turned fluid. Ben understood what it was like to be me more than anyone in the world. Having shared a womb, nothing was off-limits between us. I told Ben about the embarrassing gaffes I'd made that day, how insecure I felt in social situations, how much I missed Sloane.

When Ben's tenure at Paul Newman's camp ended, he moved to Manhattan. He rented a tiny room that fit only a bed and a bookcase, and started looking for jobs on Craigslist.

One day, visiting him at his apartment, I looked him in the eye and apologized about hooking up with Emma Ramsdale. "I'm sorry for how much I hurt you," I said.

He looked at me a second. "I need to tell you something," he said. During the years we weren't talking, he'd exacted revenge by sleeping with my ex-girlfriend from high school, Claire.

I was livid. Not only because he'd fucked my ex-girlfriend, but because he'd let me feel guilty all these years, even though he had done the same thing. I stormed out of his apartment.

But as I strode indignantly down the sidewalk, it occurred to me how silly this all was. It all seemed a lifetime ago. We had both been in so much pain. I called Ben and told him I forgave him, and I hoped he forgave me. He said he did.

One day after class I was walking down the hall when Sloane caught up with me. She asked if I wanted to walk her to the library. My heart started thudding in my chest. I said yes and walked silently next to her. I tried to act how I'd acted that day I ran into her on the street. I was quiet and courteous. When we got to the library, she said bye and went inside. I smiled the whole walk home.

The next class nothing happened. The class after that she asked me to walk her to the library again. Soon it became a regular thing. I looked forward to that walk all week.

One day at the end of our walk Sloane said, "You should come see my new apartment."

"I'd like that," I said.

She looked flustered and walked away.

I told Linda. She said she wasn't surprised that my new energy was attracting Sloane.

"She must be curious," Linda said, "about how much you've changed. Maybe it's time you sent her that letter."

I did. Sloane didn't reach out for a week. Then one day I got a text from her asking if I was free to stop by her apartment. I hit the doors of the library at a dead run.

Sloane and I sat on the couch. I felt sparks between us, but I was determined to keep my energy and certainly my hands to myself. All of a sudden she slid over on the couch, leaned in, and kissed me on the lips. I kissed her back, softly. Then she pulled away. I wanted to pull her into my arms, but I didn't. I just sat there. Then I left.

I didn't hear from her for a week. A thousand times I wanted to call her, but I didn't. I'd lie in my tiny, raised bed at night and think about that kiss. Sometimes I'd laugh out loud.

The next time I was at Sloane's, we started kissing and ended up on her bed, fully clothed. My leg was between hers, and she started grinding against it, until she had an orgasm. But I hadn't had an orgasm, and I felt like my body was going to explode. The old panicky need for her to attend to me surfaced (*It's only fair*, my mind said). But another part of me remembered what I'd learned—*focus on giving to her, rather than getting for you*—so I just lay back. After a while, Sloane said, "Are you okay? Is it okay if we don't . . ." I smiled and said it was fine. I was just happy to be there.

I think that was the last test. Something was different about me in a way that you just can't fake. Later, when we talked about it, Sloane said that being with me that night felt safe in a way that it never had before.

Two months later, I received another rejection from an investment bank. There had been more than a dozen. Only Bank of America in Charlotte was left. I'd made it to the second round of interviews but hadn't heard back. I sat dejected in the soft armchair in Sloane's studio apartment.

We were back together, though it still felt probationary. She looked up from her book and saw my glum face. She came over and sat on the arm of the chair.

"Sam," she said, "you don't see what I see. You are smart and charismatic. Someone will see that. They'll be lucky to have you."

It was the nicest thing anyone had ever said to me.

A few days later Sloane and I were sitting in her apartment when my cell phone rang. I knew it was Bank of America.

I picked up the phone and the voice said, "I am so happy to tell you that you have been accepted into the Bank of America analyst class of 2003." I leapt off the floor and pumped my fist in the air. Sloane started jumping up and down, too, both of us silent as the HR woman chattered on about start dates and starting salaries. We kept silently jumping until I hung up the phone. Then we both screamed, "Yes!"

CHAPTER 20

Protector of the Stupid

◻

In December 2002, at the age of twenty-three, I graduated from Columbia. The Bank of America job didn't start for six months, and I had to move out of the dorms and find a place to live. Sloane asked if I wanted to move in with her until she graduated in the summer.

The next six months were some of the happiest of my life. I had a dream job lined up and was with my dream girl. I moved into Sloane's studio apartment on 106th and Amsterdam and got a job waiting tables at Deluxe, an "upscale diner" on Broadway at 113th Street. Sloane went to school, I worked, and at night we'd roll her TV over and watch Lakers games in bed. I read the *Wall Street Journal* every day, and my fellow waiters would tease me, saying they'd known plenty of actors who waited tables between gigs, but never a banker. As I read about hedge fund managers or bank CEOs, I'd fantasize about someday being important enough to be in the paper myself. Sloane started talking about moving with me to Charlotte.

I spent a lot of time with Ben, who was having a harder first year of sobriety than me. He was deeply depressed; some days he could barely get out of bed. He cried often. I could hardly fathom that the guy sobbing on my shoulder was the same one who'd pulverized guys in college.

We often talked about how worried we were for our younger siblings, Daniel and Julia. They were still living with Mom and Dad; things had gotten much worse. After the split, when Daniel and Julia stayed with Mom, they had to fend for themselves. When they stayed with Dad, they had to deal with his rages and those of his girlfriend, Sara, a deeply sarcastic, easily infuriated woman. It was especially hard for Julia, the only girl in the family. That year she'd walked into a room and overheard my dad on the phone say he'd "fucked her brains out." Julia didn't know if he was talking about Sara or someone else. She'd called me, sobbing.

The effects of their fractured home life were becoming apparent. That year, at the age of sixteen, Daniel dropped out of high school. He smoked weed every day, and his weight was ballooning. Julia was also overweight. She hung out with a tough crew, got in fights, and started wearing her hair in cornrows.

After Sloane graduated in May, we flew down to Charlotte together to look at apartments. From the moment she stepped off the plane, I could tell she felt out of place. She loved fashion and culture, an LA-and-New York kind of girl. Charlotte was SimCity with fried pickles. We stayed in a motel that looked much better on the Internet than in person. One night, we were startled awake at 3:00 a.m. by a man pounding on our door, shouting. It was just a drunk who'd forgotten his room number, but when I saw Sloane's face, I knew she wasn't moving to Charlotte.

Her dad found her a job at William Morris, a major Hollywood talent agency, and she moved back to LA. I was crushed. She said she wanted to stay together, but I'd be working nonstop, even on weekends. She'd be in LA, starting a new life.

If she'd invited me to go with her to LA, I would have. It would have almost killed me to give up my job at Bank of

America, but I would have done it. But she didn't. She said we'd give long distance a try. I was heartbroken.

Before I moved to Charlotte, there was a monthlong training program at the Millennium Hotel in Manhattan. By the time I moved into the hotel, I'd been sober for a full year. I had the minibar emptied when I arrived, so there would be no temptation.

It turned out that there were over a hundred recent college graduates in the training program; Bank of America was building out their investment bank, and this was the largest analyst class on The Street. Perhaps, I noted wryly, getting a job offer hadn't been quite the accomplishment I thought.

Every day I ran three miles on the treadmill in the hotel gym before the economics, accounting, and bond math classes held in the vast conference rooms. I was an English major, and though I'd taken two finance/accounting classes senior year, most of the material was new to me.

I was intent on building relationships that would help my career. Every analyst wore a sticker with his or her name and college on it. When I saw two tall guys with MIT stickers, I decided to sit with them.

David and Grant were smart as hell and had easy smiles, but those smiles belied mean streaks, which emerged in sarcastic comments about our classmates. Sometimes, I laughed along with them; Wall Street analyst classes are peppered with suck-ups who sit at the front of the class and ask guest lecturers questions like, "Can you share with us how it is that you became so successful?" On The Street they are known as "ass-clowns," and they became easy targets for David and Grant's ridicule. But David and Grant also cast judgment when people answered math questions incorrectly. They'd look at each other and one of them would whisper, "Berkeley," or "state school," and they'd guffaw under their breath.

At first it was funny, but then it started to grate on me. I hated their smug assurance that they were the smartest guys in the room. Where did that leave me? They were both math majors; I was an English major, and though I was sure neither of them had read *The Brothers Karamazov*, here it didn't seem to matter. I had tons of questions about what we were learning, but I was too embarrassed to ask. I began to get angry at their snide comments, and finally I said something.

"Guys, take it easy," I said, after they laughed at a woman who asked the exact question I was thinking.

"Whatever," said Grant.

"There's no such thing as a stupid question," I said.

"Yes, there is," said David.

When I became direct—"You have no right to talk down to people like that"—they turned on me.

"What, are you afraid that you're like them?" David asked.

"You *are* smart, aren't you, Sam?" Grant asked.

"Maybe he's not," said David.

Grant snickered. "Is Columbia a state school?" he asked, and they both exploded into laughter.

I stared straight ahead, livid.

They held a whispered conversation and then both leaned back in their chairs.

"POTS," Grant said. "That's what we're going to start calling you, Sam. POTS."

I tried to stop myself, but I couldn't. Hating myself for needing to know, I asked, "What does POTS stand for?"

"Protector of the stupid," said Grant, and they both roared.

That night I called Linda, furious.

"Why are you so angry?" she asked.

"Because . . . these guys . . . they pick on *everyone*. I mean, who do they think they are? They are so *smug* and *self-satisfied . . .*"

"Yes, Sam, they sound like idiots. But there are a lot of idiots out there. Why are *you* so upset?" Linda asked. Linda always seemed to think my anger came from somewhere else. *Sometimes it just is what it is.*

Then I understood. David and Grant's harsh criticism reminded me of my father.

I told her how Dad would stage these kitchen-table debates between Ben and me. At stake was Dad's approval. One of my most painful memories is losing a debate with Ben about the legality of flag burning. We were seven.

"This is not about those morons; it's about you," Linda said. "This is about a belief system that your worth comes from how smart you are. You need to stop competing with everyone. These guys are not your problem. Just move seats."

So I did.

A few nights later I was in my hotel room flipping through TV channels when I came upon *Good Will Hunting*, one of my all-time favorite movies. My favorite scene happens in a Harvard bar. Ben Affleck's roughneck character is hitting on Minnie Driver, a Harvard undergrad, and lies about being a student at Harvard. A pompous Harvard grad student hears this, realizes Affleck is lying, and starts quizzing him on intellectual subjects. Just as Affleck grows embarrassed, his best friend, Matt Damon, also a roughneck but secretly a code breaker–level genius, steps in and not only answers the grad student's questions, but embarrasses *him* with his clearly superior knowledge. Matt Damon ends up with Minnie Driver's phone number. I wanted to stand up and clap every time I saw that scene.

I often felt like Affleck: not smart enough. I couldn't find the right words when I needed them; arguments that sounded good in my head were jumbled when they came out of my mouth. My biggest fantasy was that someday I'd be like Matt Damon, able to win every argument. It was one of the reasons I read so many thick books—Dostoevsky, Tolstoy, Melville, Joyce.

I'd always wanted to be the smartest guy in the room. But no matter what I accomplished, Ben always beat me. I wasn't even the smartest guy in the womb. After *Good Will Hunting* ended I turned the TV off. I suddenly understood that my need to be the smartest guy in the room wasn't a sign of strength, but of a sense of inferiority.

The last two weeks of training were devoted to accounting. I worked out every morning. In the evenings, when other analysts went out, I stayed in the hotel room and studied and talked to Ben on the phone. He was still struggling. As I listened to him cry I'd think about how maybe the toughest guys in the world are often the ones in the most pain.

On the last day of training we received the results of the accounting final we'd taken the previous day. "This is the one that counts," the HR women had said. "This is the one your bosses will see."

They walked around handing out papers. When the head of the HR department got to me, she smiled and handed me my test. "Wow, Sam, number two in the class," she said. "I didn't know you were that sharp."

I was still smiling when David walked up to me. "Man, I did not do well on that test," he said. "Ah, it doesn't matter anyways. I've already been assigned to a desk. They're creating a new position for me: structured credit trader, really complex, model-based stuff. Derivatives. Cutting-edge finance."

His words had their intended effect. I went from being pleased that I'd scored so well on the test to feeling jealous.

"That's great," I said. "Congratulations."

"Thanks, man. How'd you do on the test?" he asked, pointing to the paper I was holding by my leg.

I looked at him a second. I thought about how badly I felt when someone trumped me intellectually, and the endlessness of this competition.

"I did okay," I said, and walked away.

CHAPTER 21

The Least Cool Thing
to Order at a Bar

¤

T he weekend after I aced the accounting final at the end
of the training program, I moved down to Charlotte to
start work on the Bank of America trading floor. I bought
a two-door Dodge Neon with manual windows and a tape
deck, and rented a small apartment. Though I'd lived alone
in San Francisco, this was different. There was no pile of cocaine under the bed, no NyQuil, no robberies or fistfights. I
was starting to feel like an adult. But I was also aware of my
propensity for self-sabotage and was nervous that I'd blow
this up, too.

I was rereading Robert B. Parker's Spenser detective series,
my all-time favorite, about a tough, well-read, wisecracking
detective who quoted Keats, always won fights, and treated
his girlfriend with tremendous respect. What I loved about
Spenser was that he lived according to a rigorous internal
code. My favorite Spenser novel was *Early Autumn*, in which
Spenser rescues a scrawny, neglected young boy and takes him
to a cabin in the woods and, through a rigorous summer-long
program of exercise, reading, and manual labor, teaches him
how to become a man.

On my first day I woke at 4:00 a.m. and ran three miles on the empty, dark streets of Charlotte, then drove twenty minutes to work, my new car slipping through the night like a shark. The trading floor in Charlotte was a giant room three stories high. You entered from a balcony that ran around the perimeter of the room, overlooking the floor. To get down, you had to walk down a long stairway, in view of all the traders. I was the first person to arrive. I sat alone for half an hour, tingling with anticipation, the stillness of the air broken only by the occasional chirp of a telephone.

At six the second-year analyst arrived and showed me how to make the packets I'd hand out every morning. After the lesson was finished, I sat back down on a folding chair and watched traders stream in carrying the *Wall Street Journal* in one hand and coffee in the other. One shook my hand. Another sent me for a second cup of coffee. There was no desk for me; I was just another kid there to fetch lunch.

When Marshall Masters stepped onto the trading floor, heads turned and eyes followed him as he walked past the rows to his desk. His blond hair was graying, and he looked older than his thirty-eight years. He was tall, and though his frame was athletic, his gut strained against his shirt, evidence of years of client dinners. I walked up to him and we shook hands. He pointed to a trader in the next row and told me I'd be working for him and to introduce myself. Then he sat down to pick up the two calls that were already on hold for him.

My new boss, Richard "Hoff" Hoffstedter, was a lump of a man with intense eyes and a Wayne Newton shock of black hair, which he tended like a groundskeeper. A senior trader, Hoff was known for his maniacal precision, consistent profitability, and the occasional emotional explosion. I got to see an explosion on my first day.

Every time a corporate bond trader buys a bond, he sells

an equivalent amount of treasury bonds to hedge his interest rate risk (leaving him exposed only to credit risk—the risk the corporation will declare bankruptcy—which is what he's an expert in). That morning Hoff noticed that his corporate bond portfolio was not fully hedged. He assumed it was a clerical error made by the intern, and yelled out, "Anderson!" But Cliff Anderson wasn't there; the Friday before was the last day of his internship. Hoff called over an assistant and instructed him to check all the trades and find the error. The kettle was on, set to a simmer.

The assistant finished checking the trades and said he couldn't find an error. Hoff stared at him, his face reddening.

"Check it again," he said. "Hurry." If interest rates moved 1/10th of a percent, he'd lose $15,000. All traders dislike losing money; Hoff loathed it.

The assistant returned after rechecking the trades. This time he stood a few feet back from Hoff.

"I found the problem," he said.

"What is it?" spat Hoff.

"Anderson sold treasuries when he was supposed to buy."

"Let me see that!" Hoff screamed. As Hoff examined the trading pad, his chest started rising and falling in heavier and heavier breaths. He began to draw in air through his nose with great intensity. His face turned purple. I knew exactly what was going to happen.

"Fuck!" he screamed. He checked the price the trade had been executed at and then checked the current market price: the market had moved 1.5/10ths of a percent. He was down $150,000.

"Fuck!"

He picked up the phone, hit the direct line to the treasury desk.

"This is Hoff. Listen, I bought when I was supposed to sell. Fuck! Fuck! I need a bid on twenty million long bonds. Fuck!

Fuck!" He listened, then yelled, "Done," executing the trade. "Goddamn it!" he shouted, and slammed the phone down.

The floor was silent. Everyone watched Hoff. He sat there with his chest heaving, as if he'd just sprinted a mile. Then, suddenly, his head exploded.

"Get me Anderson!" he roared. "Get Anderson on the fucking phone RIGHT NOW."

Cliff Anderson was in all probability enjoying the high of a recently smoked joint during a leisurely drive back to Vermont. Anderson had a taste for weed and a more-than-occasional beer, I was told later, which was why he made so many mistakes.

The assistant got Anderson on the phone. Hoff picked up the line.

"Anderson, you goddamn punk. You little fucking prick. You bought bonds instead of selling. I'm down a hundred and fifty. That's more than *your life is worth*, do you hear me? Your entire life! I'd short your life *huge* at a hundred fifty thousand dollars. Where are you, in the car? Driving home? Well, I tell you what. You better keep driving. All the way, straight to Vermont. Because if I find you, if I see you again, I'm going to rip you limb from limb. Do you hear me? If I see you again, you are dead. Dead." He slammed the phone down and stalked off the floor.

Hello, Dad, I thought.

I worked like a surgery resident. Twelve to fourteen hours a day during the week, and five or six hours both days of the weekend. I created flash cards for every bond Hoff traded, so I could study all the variables that impacted the price of a bond: credit rating, deal size, call schedule. I'd review them in bed before I went to sleep. I was the first to arrive and the last to leave. Walking to my car at night my brain would throb.

Hoff was old school, so I fetched his breakfast (scrambled eggs and bacon), lunch (turkey sandwich), and Diet Dr Peppers. He'd whip out the money-clipped wad of bills from his front pants pocket and peel off a few twenties—barely making a dent—to pay for both our lunches. Traders rarely carry wallets. Wallets are too small to fit their wads of cash.

Hoff was extremely successful, and I could tell why. He was meticulous and never got distracted. He could sit silent and focused for hours at a time. Just when I thought he might never speak again, he'd lean back and scream at the top of his lungs, "OH, BID TEN MILLION BUD THIRTY-TWOS!" and I'd startle, spilling my coffee.

At the end of the day, Hoff would patiently answer all my questions, though if anyone was within earshot, he'd tease me for asking so many.

"I'm going to call you Dr. Polk," he said, "because you are painful, like a dentist."

But he took an interest in me. He encouraged me to take the CFA exams, a three-part series of once-per-year tests, the Wall Street equivalent of an MBA. He let me call him on the weekends to ask questions about bonds. For Christmas that year he brought in a dentist uniform shirt with "Dr. Polk" embroidered on the front and burst into laughter when he handed it to me. For a while I thought he might be the mentor I was looking for, but one day an incident on the trading floor changed my mind.

Traders love to bet. They'll bet on anything, especially if it involves embarrassing someone. When Hoff learned my middle name was Iverson, he offered me $500 to put my hair into cornrows. "Like Allen Iverson!" he screamed. I declined. Another guy was offered $200 if he'd eat one of everything out of the vending machines. Huge bets were placed on how many donut holes an intern could consume in an hour.

I came to understand just how much money was liable to be thrown around. One morning at ten, I was startled by a shout: "She's here! She's here!" Neil, a young trader, walked onto the balcony overlooking the floor, escorting a young woman carrying a bag. Every eye was glued to her as she walked down the stairs onto the trading floor. Neil guided her over to Hoff, who didn't look up from his monitor.

"This is him," Neil said. "This is the guy."

"Do you want me to do this here?" the woman asked.

Everyone laughed and a cheer went up.

"Right here," Neil said.

She put her bag down and spread some newspapers on the floor. Then she took out hair clippers. While Hoff continued to type, she began to shave his head. Hoff didn't look up from his screen as, clump by clump, his beloved mane fell to the floor. The entire trading floor stood to watch. When she buzzed the last clump from his head, everyone clapped and cheered. Then they sat down and went back to work. Neil handed Hoff a stack of cash.

I learned later that they were all out at a bar the night before, ribbing Hoff about how much he loved his hair. Someone asked Hoff how much it would cost for him to shave his head on the trading floor. Hoff thought about it for a second.

"Six thousand dollars," he said.

Within an hour, the traders had collected the money.

That day Hoff pocketed the price of the Dodge Neon I was driving. It was hard being new on Wall Street, seeing people throw around more money on bets than I had in my checking account.

But it wasn't just the amount of money that bothered me. I recognized their behavior as adolescent, and I was trying to grow up.

But I was also desperate to fit in. To become a full-fledged trader, instead of a coffee fetcher, I needed the traders to like me. The hardest part about the Hoff-haircut story was that the traders had been out as a group, without me. I was worried about what would happen when the traders found out I didn't drink.

A huge part of being a Wall Street trader is entertaining. Even in Charlotte, we were always going out to dinner and drinks with clients, or flying to New York to take clients to ball games.

That was one of the reasons Marshall Masters was so beloved. The only thing that approached Marshall's appetite for risk was his appetite for partying. He had a legendary night game. He was out with clients every single night—at dive bars in Charlotte, or swanky restaurants in Tribeca, having flown up to New York for the night—cocktail always in hand, until two or three in the morning. Then, he'd be at his trading desk by six. It was rumored he got two hundred text messages a day. His voice mailbox was perpetually full. He'd been a groomsman in over thirty weddings.

I was sort of the opposite of that, and being sober made things much harder. Without the liquid courage of alcohol, I had a tough time participating in conversations at client dinners. I'd sit there, mute, trying to will the waiters to clear the plates quickly so we could get the check and leave.

None of the traders had noticed yet that I didn't drink. I was worried that when they did, they might dismiss me completely.

I missed drinking, not just the joyful release of a night out, where hours flew by in a way they never did while sober, but also the comfort that came from knowing I could, with the crack of a beer can, escape from my mind. But even though I yearned for a beer, I never once considered starting up. In the year and a half I'd been sober, my internal shame and self-loathing had been replaced with something new, something that still felt awkward to me—a sense of self-respect.

One night about a month after I started working, I went out to Connolly's, a dive bar across the street from Bank of America, with the traders. TJ Johnson, an imperious frat boy from Ohio, was ordering drinks. I sidled up to the other end of the bar, hoping to quietly order my Diet Coke. He saw me.

"Mr. Polk! What can I get for you? I'm buying," he practically screamed.

I leaned toward him even though we were a good fifteen feet apart, and said, "Diet Coke, please." I was quite sure that was the least cool thing a man could order in a bar.

"What?" he yelled.

"Diet Coke," I said, a little louder.

He shook his head and cupped his hand to his ear.

"I can't hear you. Speak up!"

Just then, the bar went silent as I yelled out, "Diet Coke!" The spotlight descended.

"Diet Coke? Come on. Let me get you a *drink*," shouted TJ.

I shook my head and mumbled for the fourth time, "Diet Coke." Bewildered, he turned to the bartender and placed the order.

When the drinks were up, I went over to grab mine and he looked at me funny.

"Do you not drink?" he asked.

"I don't," I said, and walked quickly to the other side of the room. I knew my secret was out.

It spread like wildfire. The next morning Marshall was talking about taking the desk out that night for drinks. He spied me walking along the aisle and said loudly with a toothy smile, "Let's take Sam out and get him drunk!" I was too far away to respond and I watched Neil lean over and say, "Sam doesn't drink." I saw Marshall's head shake in disbelief.

"What? Sam, is this true? Do you not drink?" Marshall yelled.

The desk was silent. My worst nightmare had come true. I froze.

Marshall looked at me a second and then waved me over. I walked to his desk and squatted down next to him, hopeful that he would speak more softly if I were closer.

He was silent for a second and then asked me quietly, "Is there a reason that you don't drink that you don't want to talk about?"

I was startled but after a moment said simply but firmly, "Yes."

He looked at me as if he recognized something.

Then he said, "Okay," and turned back to his monitors.

CHAPTER 22

The Ice Melteth

◻

When Marshall reacted to the news of my not drinking with gentle respect rather than the ridicule I anticipated, I didn't know what to make of it. I walked away from that conversation grateful but puzzled.

Marshall started asking me to walk with him for coffee every couple of days. He asked questions about my family and told me stories about his. He didn't ask me directly about my drinking, but he hinted that he understood I had a history, and he was okay with that. When he was in New York, he'd call the desk and if I picked up we'd chat. I didn't think much of it, except that I was pleased I had earned the attention of the boss.

A few months later, end-of-year bonuses were given out. Because I was in the analyst program and had only been working six months, I wouldn't receive my first bonus till next August. I watched, racked with jealousy, as the traders went into a conference room and came out with bonuses several times what I'd earn that year.

Bonus time on trading floors is when personnel changes happen. Traders will wait until their bank accounts are fattened with their year-end bonuses before announcing that they've accepted new positions elsewhere. This year, the first to leave were Neil and TJ, who'd scored huge contracts with CSFB and Morgan Stanley, respectively. Neil had backed up Marshall, who was often away from his desk in risk meetings or traveling to meet with clients. So Marshall called me and asked me to serve that role, in addition to my responsibilities with Hoff. I was thrilled to be allied with two powerful men.

The next week, Hoff's desk was empty, and a trading assistant told me he'd resigned the night before. He'd never even told me he was thinking about leaving, and I felt betrayed. But I also knew this was good for me.

That afternoon, Marshall called me. "I want you to trade Hoff's sectors until we find a replacement," he said. "It's temporary, but it's a big opportunity. Are you ready, Sammy?" he asked. No one had ever called me Sammy before, but Marshall had started to, and I sort of liked it.

It seemed crazy that Marshall wanted me to become a trader so soon. First-year analysts were almost never allowed to trade. Traders worked with hundreds of millions of dollars a day. The risks were simply too big. There were guys on The Street still fetching coffee in their fourth year. I felt like a nurse being asked to perform heart surgery.

No, I thought. "Yes," I said.

"I want you to call me five, six times a day," Marshall said. "Ask all the questions you come up with. I am going to teach you how to trade."

All of a sudden grown men were screaming at me, people were calling me from London, and I wasn't fetching anyone's coffee. I spent hours every night writing out what I would say on the morning call that was broadcast over loudspeakers in London, New York, Charlotte, Chicago, and Los Angeles, so I might sound like I knew what I was talking about. While the other traders spoke from memory, I hid a piece of lined notebook paper on my lap with my entire speech written out.

I made some mistakes, but Marshall supported me. A few

times I heard salesmen complain about me to Marshall. Marshall said, "Give him time, just you watch," and never said a word to me about it.

When Marshall was in New York, I'd speak to him on the phone a dozen times a day. Usually the calls lasted ten seconds or less—the rapid-fire staccato traders learn to speak in—but at the end of the day, he'd take a few minutes to teach me trading protocol or tell me stories about being a young trader himself.

After a month or so, I was getting the hang of trading, so when Marshall called to tell me he was moving a senior trader over to work with me, I was crushed.

"Haven't I been doing a good job?" I asked.

"Yes," he said. "You did great. You're going to learn a ton from McMahon."

"Why are you taking this away from me?" I asked.

He let out an exasperated snort. Then he paused.

"Sam," he said, "this is *good* for you. Trust me."

"What if McMahon takes all the sectors and doesn't let me trade?" I said.

"He's the senior guy, Sam," he said, gently but firmly. "What he says, goes. I fetched coffee for three years when I started on Wall Street."

I set the phone down and stared across the trading floor at Brendan McMahon with the hostility of a stepchild. Brendan was a trim, clean-cut thirty-five-year-old. UNC Business School graduates didn't often make it into Wall Street firms, but Brendan had cold-called Marshall, and Marshall liked him. Brendan was quiet and humble, more blue-collar than white-collar.

That first day Marshall told us we'd be working together, McMahon pulled me into an office. "We have six sectors to split up," he said. "I'm going to let you trade the two smallest ones."

I guess he doesn't realize he could just tell me to get him coffee.

"I know I don't have to give you any sectors, but I've been watching you," he said. "You're young but talented. I think we are going to make great partners."

I was relieved. Brendan looked regretful. "I'm sorry I couldn't give you one of the bigger sectors. This is a big shot for me," he said. "I hope you understand."

I did understand. I was surprised he was letting me keep any sectors. Letting go of even two small sectors meant a step down in profile for Brendan and would likely impact his end-of-year bonus.

That he let me keep two sectors surprised me. What he did two hours later shocked me. He came by my desk, tapped my shoulder, and pointed to the office we'd spoken in earlier.

When I sat down across from him, he said, "I'm sorry. I was being selfish. We're going to be partners. I'm going to help you like I wish someone had helped me. We'll split the sectors down the middle, even steven."

I almost laughed out loud, marveling at my good fortune. Then my throat grew thick. I nodded a thank-you to Brendan, afraid that if I spoke I'd start crying in gratitude.

For the next few months, I poured everything I had into trading. I read incessantly about the chemicals and metals/mining sectors I traded, and spent evenings and weekends in the office doing extra work and studying for the CFA. Brendan and I had been reserved with each other at first, but now we laughed and joked all day long. Sometimes we played golf together on the weekends.

I thought about Sloane all the time and called her often. At first, she called me back right away. But as the months passed, she started taking longer and longer to return my calls. I'd leave casual, happy-sounding messages so that she'd want to call me back. What I really felt like doing, though, was begging her to come back.

I woke up early on the Saturday morning of my first CFA test. I'd been studying for six months. The pass rate was only 30 percent. The phone rang at 6:00 a.m. It was Marshall.

"Sammy," Marshall said when I picked up, "I wanted to call and say I'm thinking about you today. If anyone can pass this test on the first try, it's you."

"How did you even know it was today?" I blurted out.

"Are you kidding?" he said. "I wouldn't have missed it." He said that even though the pass rate was so low and the six-hour test so grueling, he had total faith in me.

My dad missed *birthdays*, but here was Marshall, rising at dawn just to support me taking a test.

Then one day, Marshall asked me to drive him to the airport and then drop his car off at a mechanic. On the way, he asked me how things were going.

I had learned how to answer that question from my father. In our house it was never enough to say you needed something; you had to *prove* it. Marshall was in charge of my bonus, so I took the same tack with him.

"Things are tough right now," I said. "I'm working late every night. I'm already studying for the next CFA test. Nights *and* weekends. Money is tight. I'm not getting any support from my parents, and I have serious student loans and credit card debt."

Money *was* tight, but not because I wasn't being paid enough. I was making $55,000 a year—meager for Wall Street, but plenty for a recent college grad. But I was paying off student loans, a twice-a-week counselor, and a large credit card balance I'd built up during college.

Marshall looked over at me and then opened the center console between us. Inside were stacks of hundred-dollar bills. He pulled out a stack and held it in my direction.

"Take it," he said.

My eyes bulged as I stared at the kind of money I had only

dreamed about. Then I looked up at the kind of man I had only dreamed about. He smiled at me.

I knew I couldn't take it. But I was so touched that I couldn't even speak. I put my hands up in a gesture of refusal. I knew I had overstated my case, and anyway, I wanted to do it myself.

He put the money back in the console and then looked over at me with a serious expression. And then he said the words I had waited my whole life to hear.

"Sam," he said, "if you ever really need money—like, if you ever need a hundred thousand dollars—just call me. No questions asked. I trust you."

We were just pulling into the airport, and I waited till he got out of the car before I started to cry. At first it was just tears blurring my vision as I cut across the empty Charlotte freeway. But soon it turned into deep, heaving sobs and I had to pull off to the shoulder.

CHAPTER 23

The Ephemeral Prison

◻

That moment when Marshall offered me $100,000
changed everything. It wasn't about the money. I didn't
need $100,000; I needed someone to tell me I was worth being
taken care of.

I walked with my head held higher. I slept better. I started
to feel like things would work out, like I wouldn't have to
scratch and claw to survive. And slowly I started to trust my
instincts when it came to trading. But change happens on the
margin. I still carried with me the propensity to self-destruct.

In June, the metals and mining sector that I traded leapt into
the news. Western Mining, a small ore producer in Australia,
was the target of a three-way bidding war. The two largest
metals companies in the world—BHP and Rio Tinto—along
with a smaller Brazilian company called CVRD, were looking to acquire Western Mining.

When a company gets acquired, the debt of that company
becomes the debt of the acquiring company. I traded the debt
(or bonds) of Western Mining, so whoever won the bidding
war would take over that debt. If BHP or Rio—both with
sterling credit profiles—bought the company, Western Mining bonds would increase in value. But if CVRD—an already
debt-laden company in a risky economy—won the bidding

war, Western Mining bonds would plummet. When the head-lines hit, Western Mining bonds dropped precipitously.

I read everything I could about the industry—newspaper articles, CEO speeches, tax filings. I printed out each compa-ny's annual report and took them home at night. I spoke to the metals analyst at Bank of America.

I hadn't understood how investors knew whether bonds were going to go up or down. This time, I saw the trade. Though it was unlikely that CVRD would win this bidding war, their involvement frightened investors. That created an opportunity: Western Mining bonds were trading so low that if either BHP or Rio won the bidding war, Western Mining bonds would skyrocket. Of course, if CVRD somehow did win, the bonds would fall even further. But I was confident that I had thought it through, and I started to buy bonds.

At first I bought $20 million worth, a healthy size for a position. Then I typed up a message about why I was buying them and sent it to the sales force so they could try to sell some of my bonds at a profit. Instead of finding another buyer, I found another seller. A senior salesman asked me if I wanted to buy $40 million more in bonds.

"Yes," I said, before I really thought about it. The size of my Western Mining position was no longer healthy; it was scary, especially for a rookie trader. Eventually, the risk monitors would discover how many bonds I owned, but that would take a few days. I knew the position was too big, so I leaned over and told Brendan I owned $60 million in Western Mining bonds, and why.

He nodded. "Go for it," he said.

The next day, I got a phone call from a trader at a hedge fund who'd heard I was buying Western Mining bonds.

"This is our favorite trade, Sam," he said. "Unfortunately, we have to sell some bonds because we're closing down one of our funds. Do you want them?"

My stomach clenched. I already had a huge position. But I didn't want him to think I was scared. *Fuck it.* "Sure," I said. "I'll take them."

Buying $100 million in Western Mining bonds was a *holy shit* proposition. When I hung up the phone, I just sat there, numb and mute. I knew I should tell Brendan, but he'd want to know why I'd added more. I didn't really know the answer. It dawned on me that with a position this size I'd be fired if I was wrong. Brendan, too. I was also hit with a rush of adrenaline that I hadn't felt in years, the same rush that came with getting in a fight, or scoring a big bag of cocaine.

The risk reward of the trade was not in my favor. If BHP or Rio Tinto bought Western Mining, I'd probably make $1 or $2 million. If CVRD bought them, I'd lose $5 or $10 million in minutes. When Brendan returned to the desk, I didn't look at him.

The next day was a Friday, and the morning passed without a headline about Western Mining. In the afternoon I caught a plane to Denver. I was on my way to visit Ben.

We'd been sober almost two years. We talked on the phone two or three times a day. Everyone on the trading desk knew Ben because he called so often. In his first year of sobriety, Ben had worked a series of odd jobs, barely making ends meet. When he lived in that tiny room in New York, he'd been too poor to afford a winter coat. One night at an AA meeting, a woman noticed he didn't have a coat and took him to the Gap and bought him a fur-lined leather jacket, which got him through the winter.

But things were looking up for Ben. He'd never been as focused on money as I was, but he'd decided he wanted the security of a steady paycheck. Three years out of college, he'd managed to talk his way into the analyst class of the consulting giant Bain & Company, working in their Boston headquarters. A job at Bain carried prestige. I was happy for him and a little jealous.

On the plane to Denver my mind started racing about the Western Mining position. *What if CVRD wins? What if I'm wrong?* My stomach tied itself into knot after knot. *I could lose $20 million.* My hands were cold, clammy. Rivulets of sweat skied down my back.

By the time I landed I was nauseous. I must have looked green, because when Ben saw me, his smile vanished.

"What's wrong?" he asked.

Part of me didn't want to tell him my job was in jeopardy. But he was, as he'd always been, the single most comforting presence in times of stress. During the drive to the cabin I told him the whole story. I finished as we arrived. A few minutes later, standing in the kitchen of our cabin, he said, "Dude, why don't you tell Marshall?"

"No way," I said.

Ben looked at me a second. "You're doing it again," he said softly.

"What?" I asked, suddenly furious. "What am I doing again?"

He looked sad. "The same thing you did at Columbia. The same thing you did at ON24. The same thing you did with Sloane. The same thing you did when you hooked up with Emma in high school. It's self-sabotage; don't you understand? Why are you risking everything you've worked for? Why are you keeping it a secret? Why don't you ask for help?"

I sat quietly in my chair as I thought about what Ben said. I thought about those moments after I got suspended or fired, how ashamed I felt. I thought about the pain of Sloane dumping me, and my estrangement from my brother. I didn't want to go through any of that again. Still, the thought of opening up—making myself vulnerable—to Marshall was terrifying.

Ben watched me. "It sounds like you have a good relationship with Marshall," he said. "It sounds like your trade makes sense. Why don't you just ask him for advice?"

My mind flashed on Marshall's toothy smile as he held out stacks of hundred-dollar bills to me. I also remembered what Marshall had told me about his own career.

What Marshall had recognized in me was his own checkered past. He hadn't, he told me on one of our walks, left Merrill Lynch voluntarily. As the youngest managing director in firm history, he'd felt tremendous pressure to perform. He hadn't taken a day off in five years. "I lost perspective," he said. After one of his positions went bad, he'd tried to make up the losses. He'd started secretly betting on interest rates. He took positions in treasury futures, a type of derivative that let him keep his trades off the books. He built a massive position—billions of dollars of exposure, multiples bigger than his biggest corporate bond trades. Soon the position started going against him. He doubled down. He started hiding his trading tickets, a fireable offense in those days (these days you'd go to prison).

One morning at 3:00 a.m. he startled awake. He rubbed sleep from his eyes and used the remote to turn on the TV. There'd been a coup in Nigeria. Marshall was betting that treasury futures would fall. Anytime there is global unrest—like a coup in Nigeria—treasuries rally as investors seek safety. Marshall turned to the woman next to him in bed, who was now awake. "Today will be my last day at Merrill Lynch," he said. He'd been right. His firing had made headlines. Marshall Masters knew plenty about bad positions.

I looked at Ben and then went into the bathroom and sat on the toilet. Before I lost my nerve, I dialed Marshall's number and held my breath.

"Sammy?" he said when he picked up. "It's Saturday. What's up?"

"I've got a problem," I began.

"Let's hear it," he said.

I told him everything: the various trades, the thought

process, the size of my position. When I finished, I held my breath, waiting for the gigantic hand to slam down on me. Waiting for the rage I knew was building. Waiting for the kettle to scream.

Marshall waited a few beats. "That's a big position," he said. "But I like it. Let's keep it. I like your instincts. Keep trusting them." Then he hung up.

A few weeks later, headlines blared across the tape: *BHP to Buy Western Mining*.

For the first time in my career, my portfolio made over a million dollars in a day.

CHAPTER 24

Charleston

◻

That year, down in Charlotte, I received a bonus, $40,000, and for the first time in my life, I had a cushion. I no longer needed to check my balance at the ATM, or wait for a paycheck to pay my bills.

A few times that year, Marshall brought me down to Charleston with a few of the more senior traders; they golfed while I studied for the CFA in the hotel, and at night we went to dinners at The Oak, the steak house Marshall had just opened. After dinner, I walked alone along the quiet, leafy streets, my stomach full and my head proud that I had been invited to one of the places rich people keep secret.

I invited Dad to spend a weekend with me in Charleston. I wanted to try and improve our relationship, which had been strained ever since I got sober. We talked on the phone less. When we saw each other, there was a tension between us that hadn't been there before he'd drunk that Manhattan. He'd called me out of the blue one day to tell me that he'd just gotten married to Sara, the woman he'd left my mom for.

"Why didn't you tell me?" I'd said.

"I knew you'd be upset," he said. "And I didn't want that to ruin it."

Linda said I deserved to be treated with respect by everyone, even my dad. I told her I wanted Dad in my life no matter what. Maybe we could start working on a new way of being together. I had money now, and so did he. A few years ago he'd taken a job at the firm of one of his clients, a technology company, and now he was an executive. He wasn't rich, but for once he wasn't living paycheck to paycheck, either.

When Dad arrived, I took him golfing. I'd learned to play over the past year. Marshall said I had a natural stroke. I was excited for Dad to see how good I'd gotten. I also thought golf might replace drinking as the thing we did for fun together.

Dad couldn't hit a straight shot. Sometimes he missed the ball completely. "Keep your head down," I counseled.

"Fuck," he yelled. He looked embarrassed, then angry. Halfway through the round he quit.

At lunch that day I told him how I'd become a trader after only eight months, and how much my bonus was. "I'm proud of you," he said. "I knew if I sent you to Columbia, things would work out."

I'd been waiting for Dad to say he was proud of me my whole life; his words felt like salve on a wound. But I also felt a momentary annoyance—it seemed he was taking some of the credit.

That night, we sat across from each other at a seafood restaurant with linen tablecloths. I started telling him about sobriety, about how I was trying to live a different kind of life. I talked about my relationship with Marshall, how he had offered me $100,000 with no conditions.

"Marshall said he trusted me," I said. "He said he'd give me money just because I asked for it."

My father grew quiet. He rested his fork on his plate.

"You ungrateful shit," Dad said.

"That's not what I meant, Dad . . ." I started. But he was livid. He didn't talk to me for the rest of the meal. Eventually the waiter brought the check. He paid. We left.

For years I had a recurring dream about my father. In the dream I'm chasing him. I'm furious. I try to punch him, but my hands feel heavy and slow. I can't connect. Even when I do, the punches glance off, don't hurt him. I had that dream every night for a week after I got back from Charleston.

A few weeks later I was looking for a research report in the trading intranet, when I came across a document entitled *CDS vs. Bonds—Compensation Comparison*. I looked around to make sure no one could see my monitor. I knew I wasn't supposed to open this file, but I double-clicked. It was an analysis comparing recent bond trader contracts to CDS trader contracts.

The Great Gatsby's Nick Carraway was a bond salesman, which is to say that bonds have been around a long time. CDSs (credit default swaps, also called credit derivatives) were brand-new. They were essentially insurance policies on companies. You paid a quarterly fee, but if the company went bankrupt, you'd be fully compensated for the losses.

There were two key differences between CDSs and bonds. If you wanted to buy a million dollars' worth of bonds, you had to invest a million dollars. But with CDSs, if you wanted a million-dollar insurance policy on a company, you hardly had to put up any money at all—leverage. And whereas there was a finite amount of bonds, the amount of CDSs that could exist was infinite. A company might only have $100 million in bonds outstanding, but there might be billions of dollars' worth of insurance policies written on those bonds. CDSs were, in short, a sophisticated way for people to gamble without putting up any money.

Back when CDSs were being invented, macho, athletic bond traders dominated trading floors. They hardly noticed the math and physics majors hiding in the corners, working on Excel spreadsheets, quietly creating the new CDS market.

Even as late as 2001, when I was an intern at CSFB, bond traders were the nucleus of the business.

That soon changed. In 2003, the year I started at Bank of America, CDS volumes eclipsed bonds. Soon they weren't in the same ballpark. CDS traders began to generate huge profits. They were smarter, younger, and more profitable. They spoke in a complex language bond guys couldn't understand. Power shifted; CDS traders now stood in the center of the floor. Bond traders went from being lions to dinosaurs in the blink of an eye.

The figures I saw on my screen showed bond trader contracts guaranteeing salaries of $750,000 to $1 million per year. I'd been shocked when I learned that traders just a few years ahead of me earned that kind of money.

The document showed that CDS traders made twice as much, earning $1.5 million to $2 million per year. Some had two-year guarantees.

I looked up to see Brendan returning to the desk from the bathroom, and I closed the document. The week before, Brendan and his wife had invited me over for dinner. I left his house radiating gratitude for our new friendship. Now I saw Brendan with a different eye. Brendan was no CDS trader.

It wasn't just about the money. It was about where you stood in the Wall Street hierarchy. I wanted to be at the top. When I told Linda about it, she asked if I thought my desire to become a CDS trader had anything to do with my dad. "What do you mean?" I asked.

"Fantasies come from a wound," she said. "If you feel powerless, you'll create a fantasy where you have absolute power. What you really need is not to achieve the fantasy, but to heal the wound."

I told her it wasn't a fantasy. There was a very real difference between $1 million and $2 million per year. "Haven't

I healed the wound, anyways?" I asked. I'd told her how I cried after Marshall had offered me the money. I knew I'd been processing pain from my childhood, from my father, from OJ.

"You've started," she said. "This work can take a lifetime."

I wanted to be a CDS trader, but Bank of America didn't traffic in CDSs. So I read everything I could—research reports, primers, books on credit derivatives—and kept my eyes open for an opportunity.

A few months later, Marshall started a new CDS trading group and hired a thirty-year-old named Alexei Lutov to lead it.

Alexei was based in Manhattan, so he flew down to Charlotte to meet the bond traders. His reputation preceded him. He owned two Ferraris. He wore thousand-dollar pinstriped suits. On the weekends he partied on the New York club scene—models and bottles. His contract was rumored to be a "2 by 2," which meant he'd been guaranteed $2 million a year for two years. He was tall, red haired, and unhealthy looking, like skin draped loosely over a skeleton.

The bond traders took him out to a local bar known for its fried pickles and Ping-Pong table. I sipped Diet Coke and chatted with Brendan, watching Alexei out of the corner of my eye. When he was alone, I hurried over and introduced myself.

"I'm really glad to meet you," I said. "I was excited to hear you'd been hired. I'd heard so much about you." I told him I worked with Brendan McMahon and traded industrial bonds.

"So," Alexei said, a smile playing on his thin lips, "how's bond trading in Charlotte?"

I picked up on the subtle reference to *Liar's Poker*, in which Michael Lewis described "Equities in Dallas" as the worst place a young Wall Street trader could find himself. He was slicing my job.

I smiled and shrugged my shoulders. "It's a good place to start," I said. "They let me trade after eight months, so . . ."

"Eight months," he said. "That's faster than I started trading."

We stood there a moment. I saw Marshall across the bar. When I caught his eye, he lifted his glass.

Alexei saw it, too. "You and Marshall close?" he asked. His eyes were searching. I realized he was eager to impress Marshall. If I could position hiring me as beneficial to his relationship with Marshall, he might bite.

"Marshall hired me right out of Columbia," I said. "One of his best friends mentored me at CSFB. I've been Marshall's junior guy for over a year now. He's almost like a father to me."

Alexei was quiet. "Columbia," he finally said. I knew Alexei had two degrees from Columbia.

After a moment, I turned to face him. "I've been reading a lot about CDSs. One day I'd like to trade both bonds and CDSs."

Very few traders trafficked in both products; usually it was one or the other. I believed that traders of the future would be dexterous in both.

"Interesting," he said. "How long are you planning to stay in Charlotte?"

"I miss New York," I said.

The next day at noon Alexei came by my desk. When I stood, Brendan looked up and said, "Where are you going?"

"To lunch with Alexei," I said, my face growing hot.

Brendan looked at me a long moment. "Got it," he said.

I spent the next week in phone conversations with Marshall and Alexei. When it was settled, I called Brendan and asked if I could swing by his house.

When I got there, he seemed to know what I was going to say.

"I figured. I'll miss you, man. I really loved being partners with you," he said.

The day I left, Brendan came over and spent three hours helping me pack up my U-Haul. I left a big pile of thrift-store furniture on the front lawn. As I pulled away, Brendan stood next to the pile, waving.

CHAPTER 25

The Land of
Ambition and Success

❍

Alexei and I became trading partners in New York. He was nice to me—he gave me a brand-new golf club my first week—but I disliked him from the beginning. Brendan traded with an old-school ethic; if a trade went against him, he never complained. In contrast, Alexei whined and wheedled whenever a trade went bad. He'd stand over the salesman, bemoaning the money he'd lost and making empty threats about future business. His voice began to grate on me like nails on a chalkboard, which was unfortunate because now we spent twelve hours a day next to each other.

I missed Brendan. I missed sitting with my friend. But it was a matter of priorities. I got from Alexei exactly what I wanted. I became an expert in CDSs, and Alexei let me trade the telecom sector, one of the most high-profile sectors in the market.

My focus turned to finding a big trade that would establish me as a major player on Wall Street. Soon, I saw my opportunity.

A month after I moved back to New York, Verizon announced the largest single telecom-bond issuance in history.

Most bond issues are between $500 million and $1.5 billion in size. Verizon intended to borrow $4 billion with a single bond issue. Bank of America was the lead bank, and I was the lead telecom trader, which meant I would trade the new deal.

Trading a new bond deal is like being onstage opening night. The lead banker announces the exact minute the deal will become "free to trade," and as that moment approaches, the eyes of the market turn toward the trader. In the seconds before trading opens, the market seems to hold its breath. When it's time, the trader sends out an electronic message with the opening prices to the entire market and yells those prices over the loudspeaker broadcast across the entire trading floor. Then, all hell breaks loose.

The first day a bond is issued, the trading volume in that bond is usually higher than it will ever be again, and sometimes price changes can be dramatic. If there's overwhelming demand for a new bond—that is, if the market is strong and the interest rate is high—the bond price can ratchet materially higher, leaving the company furious at its bankers for charging them too high an interest rate. If the market is weak and the interest rate is too low, bonds can fall precipitously, leaving investors down money ("in the red") and furious.

The day of the Verizon deal, tensions ran high. Under Marshall Masters's leadership, Bank of America had recently become the number one–ranked investment grade trading desk on Wall Street, and this record-breaking bond deal would cement our position. That morning the market weakened unexpectedly and the bankers were worried about whether they could drum up $4 billion in orders. The bankers were led by Jeff Ponder, a former marine with a jaw that could slice apples. Ponder's reputation was at stake, as was Marshall Masters's (as was mine, though I didn't really have one). Marshall's face was serious when he pulled me aside after the deal was announced.

"I'm going to help you trade it," he said.

"I can handle it," I snapped, afraid I wasn't going to get credit. "This is my shot."

Marshall looked at me. "I know, Sammy. I'm just going to sit next to you and help if you need it."

Late in the afternoon, the Verizon deal was struggling. Investors typically receive only a fraction of their orders—they submit an order for $50 million worth of new bonds but expect to only receive $15 million. But the aggregate orders on the Verizon deal were barely over $4 billion, so the bankers would have to completely fill every order. Investors were going to receive far more bonds than they anticipated. The market had dropped that day, which makes investors nervous. They'd be downright scared when they received full allocations of Verizon bonds. Everyone would be a seller.

Once the selling began it might not stop. Hedge funds can sense weakness; if an investment looks vulnerable, they sell bonds until the market is overwhelmed and the deal goes into free fall. Then, at much lower prices, the hedge funds will buy back the bonds they've sold, netting a handsome profit.

At 2:30 p.m. I stood with Marshall and Ponder. I felt like a wide-eyed kid finally allowed at the adult table. Marshall finished telling Ponder about the market weakness. Ponder's brow furrowed.

"This is what you have to do, Ponder . . ." Marshall began.

"Don't fucking tell me what I have to do!" Ponder barked. "This is my goddamned deal!" A thick snake of a vein throbbed on his taut neck. Heads turned. We were silent. Ponder's outburst had confirmed the precarious reality of our situation.

Marshall flashed a toothy smile. "I have an idea," he said.

His strategy was risky. He wanted to open the deal *lower* than where it was priced. Investors, losing money at the outset, would be furious. But no one likes to sell at a loss. Marshall believed that opening the new issue at lower levels would stem the initial selling and bring in discount buyers. If enough buyers came in, the bond would have upward momentum when it finally reached issue price and just might close up on the day.

After thinking for a minute, Ponder grudgingly assented, although he insisted the first trade occur at issue price, to save face. Marshall nodded. As he and I walked back to the desk he asked, "Do you realize how important this is?"

I nodded. If this deal traded poorly, no company would trust us to trade marquee new deals, and we'd lose our number one ranking. Not only would that mean less prestige—it would also mean less money.

I looked at the clock—3:57 p.m. Issue price was 99.75.[1] I typed up a message to send out to the sales force that read, "Verizon new issue, opening 99.75-99.875."[2] Marshall sat next to me, both of us silent, feeling the electricity of anticipation. My hands tingled. I cracked my knuckles. At 3:59 I put my hand over the Send key and looked at Marshall. He smiled.

The clock suddenly blared 4:00. I hit Send, stood up, picked up the phone handset, which served as a microphone, and yelled, "New Verizon, opening at issue price 99.75-99.875."

The room erupted. Every salesman was on their feet with a phone pressed to each ear; the lights of the phone turret lit up. Four salesmen tried at once to sell me bonds. I told the one closest to me I would take $10 million and told the others the market had moved. I shouted into the loudspeaker, "Verizon bonds going down; the new market is 99.5-99.625."

1 Bond prices are quoted in percentages. So, 99.75 means for every thousand dollars' worth of bonds, the price is $997.50. For ten thousand dollars' worth of bonds, the price is $9,975, and so on.

2 This is a market, which means clients can transact on both sides. The left side, 99.75, is the bid side, or the price I would pay someone who was selling their bonds. The right side, 99.875, is the offer side, or the price that investors who were looking to buy would have to pay.

It'd already been loud, but when I dropped the price of the bonds, the noise ratcheted higher. I was offering to sell bonds below where the new issue priced. Investors had just spent $4 billion and were immediately down money. Salesmen were getting screamed at by their clients and were in turn screaming at me.

"Are you kidding me? Below issue price?" yelled a salesman.

"What the fuck, Polk? What the fuck?" screamed a saleswoman.

"This is unbelievable," hollered the head of sales. "Where the fuck is Marshall Masters?"

Marshall was sitting next to me. He had two phones pressed to his ears as he listened to brokers telling him where bonds were trading in the street.[3] He had a big smile across his face. The entire market was focused on this bond; Goldman Sachs, Morgan Stanley, Lehman Brothers—everyone was trading it. The volumes were enormous.

"I'm putting a 99.375 bid in the street," Marshall said to me coolly. That was a far lower price than I was paying to our accounts. If Marshall got hit, that meant that other firms were getting sold a ton of bonds and were capitulating.

So far no one had been willing to take a loss. Accounts hadn't come in to sell after I dropped the price. And then, they did.

"I got Cornerstone here, would sell you twenty million at 99.5," yelled one salesman.

"Done," I yelled back.

"I got Red River here; they wanna hit you on twenty million more down there," yelled another.

"Done," I yelled back. I'd collected over $50 million in new Verizon bonds. There was nothing but sellers.

---

3 Investment banks trade with each other through interdealer brokers, and those trades are referred to as "in the street."

"I got Sharktooth here; they are a seller of twenty million at your bid price," yelled a gray-haired, shark-faced salesman. Sharktooth was a predator; the fact that they were selling meant they smelled blood and were attacking. They would be selling bonds to every firm on The Street, hoping to effect capitulation. And it started to happen: Marshall yelled out, "We're getting hit from the street at 99.375."

I picked up the hoot and screamed out, "Verizon down again! New market: 99.375-99.5." Bonds were now offered a full quarter point cheaper than where they were issued. If buyers were out there, this might draw them in. But so far it hadn't. The selling continued. Anyone who was selling down here was losing real money.

"Polk, Grandview is looking to sell ten million at 99.375."

"Done!" I yelled again.

I now owned $100 million in Verizon bonds. I had two assistants next to me furiously scribbling the details of every trade. Their heads never lifted.

I tersely whispered to Marshall, "We're getting hit by everyone. What the fuck are we going to do?"

He looked up at me with a gleam in his eye. "I just bought seventy million from the street."

I whirled toward him. "Are you fucking kidding me?"

We were now long $170 million in bonds, the biggest position by far that I had ever had. We had exploded over our risk limits. We couldn't look down.

But Marshall wasn't worried. He was loving this.

"*Lock yourself*," he hissed. He must have sensed a pause in the selling. Locking yourself meant telling the market you will buy *or* sell bonds at the same price. It was, I realized, a brilliant idea. Traders usually make money by buying at one price and selling slightly higher. Locking myself was a signal to investors that I wasn't taking a commission, so if they came in to buy bonds now, they'd be getting a deal.

It was a last-gasp plea for buyers. If we got hit on more bonds, we'd have to take the market down again. We couldn't buy any more bonds to support the price. We'd only be able to watch as the deal puked.

I pounded out a message. "Verizon new issue, 99.375 lock!!" I hit Send, then stood and shouted into the microphone, "Ninety-nine and three-eights lock; come and get 'em!"

There was no reaction, only stunned quiet. Salesmen glared at me as they waited for their accounts to digest the fact that their new bonds had tanked. Investors were furious.

I saw the Sharktooth wire light up. They'd be sellers. I looked hard at the salesman who covered them, silently imploring him not to pick up. But he did.

"Sharktooth is a seller of twenty million more," he yelled.

I didn't say anything. I'd just sent out a market, and protocol obligated me to honor both sides of that market. If I didn't buy Sharktooth's bonds, I'd lose face. I couldn't buy any more bonds. I just stood there, as if I hadn't heard. Seconds passed.

Suddenly, the head of sales stood up. "I've got a buyer of twenty million at 99.375," he said.

"Sold to you," I yelled. To the Sharktooth salesman I made an I'll-take-them gesture. I'd bought and sold $20 million in bonds at the same price. I hadn't made any money, but at least I was still in the game. I picked up the hoot. "Buyer comes in at 99.375! I have more for sale there!"

Nothing happened. A minute passed.

Then another salesman yelled, "I'll take twenty million at 99.375." I was locking in a loss; I'd purchased most of the bonds I owned at higher prices. But I needed to build momentum.

All of a sudden, I felt the energy shift. Salesmen were listening intently into their phones. I could feel accounts sniffing around, wondering if we'd bottomed. I decided to make a ballsy move.

I stood up and shouted into the loudspeaker, "Ninety-nine point five lock. The market moves *up*." Out of the corner of my eye I saw Marshall nod.

By locking myself at a higher price, I was making a statement of confidence that the momentum had shifted. I kept a poker face, knowing that I owned $170 million in Verizon bonds. If someone came in to sell bonds here, I'd have to drop the market back down. All hope for a rally would be lost.

I saw Chuck Henry, a salesman who covered major hedge funds, stand up two rows away. I held my breath as I saw him take the phone from his ear. The fate of this deal, I knew, lay in what his accounts were going to do now.

Chuck was a wizened veteran. He knew how important this was. He stared at me for a second, expressionless. Then his face broke out in a smile. "I've got a buyer," he finally screamed. "I'll take ten million at 99.5."

"Done," I yelled over the hoot. "I'd sell ten million more at 99.5," I yelled. "Then I'm jacking the price up."

"I'll take 'em," someone yelled from across the room, and that was it. Momentum was crucial on a new deal, and it was now all going the right way. I moved the market up to 99.625, and another buyer came in.

"Ninety-nine point seven five lock," I yelled out. Back to issue bid. The bankers standing over at the side of the floor looked visibly relieved. Another buyer came in.

After I sold him bonds, I yelled out, "New market, 99.875-100!" The market seemed exhausted; no one responded. I was bidding higher than issue price, and no one was selling.

At five o'clock I totaled up the trades. Marshall and I had traded over a billion dollars of bonds. We sat there, drained, as people came up and congratulated us. *Thank God for Marshall*, I thought. I also knew the whole market had watched me trade the Verizon deal. I now had a big-time reputation on Wall Street.

A few weeks later when Marshall told me my bonus that year was $70,000, I didn't complain even though it was far below what other traders made. I was in the three-year analyst program, which meant my pay was capped. I'd earn the same as my classmates, who were still fetching coffee. I left Marshall's office and hovered by the watercooler. An analyst whom I'd been friendly with came over.

"How did your bonus talk go?" he asked.

"Fine," I said.

"That's great," he said. "Did you hear that David got promoted early?"

"That's great," I forced out and then turned away quickly so he wouldn't see my face burn with jealousy. David, the MIT guy who had made fun of me, called me protector of the stupid, had been promoted *early*? I was furious at Alexei, and especially at Marshall. He must have known David was getting promoted. Why hadn't he fought for me to get promoted, too?

After the Verizon deal, I'd thought I was the youngest, hottest trader in the market. Part of me knew that David's promotion didn't take away from my success. But another part of me was devastated. I daydreamed about being president of the United States, not vice president. I seethed with impotent rage.

This isn't over, I thought. *I'll show them what a mistake they just made.* But deep inside, in a place I didn't want to look at, I was afraid. Afraid that David was just smarter than me. Afraid I'd never earn as much money as him. Afraid I'd come in second, as I had my whole life. Afraid I'd never get the recognition I so profoundly craved.

CHAPTER 26

A Castle on a Cloud

¤

A few months after the Verizon trade, I was alone in my apartment when my phone buzzed. It was my dad. We hadn't spoken since the trip to Charleston.

"Hey Dad," I said.

"Sit down," he said. "I've got some news."

I sat. "What's up?" I said.

"We sold the company," he said. "I'm a millionaire. A multi-millionaire. A multi-multi-millionaire."

I was shocked. Dad had been talking about his stock options in the company—a tech firm that processed legal documents for litigation—for years. I thought it was just another pipe dream.

"How much did you make?" I asked.

He paused for effect. "Fifteen million dollars," he said.

I was glad I was sitting down. I had no idea *the company* was worth that much, let alone my dad's stake in it.

I knew immediately what a huge deal this was for Dad. In a single instant, all of his fantasies were realized, all his dreams fulfilled. "Dad, congratulations. I'm so happy for you."

"Thank you," he said. "You know how much this means to Sara and me."

Sara. My stomach tightened. "Dad," I said, "how much does Mom get?"

Mom and Dad had been divorced three years, after being married for twenty-five. Mom had paid Dad's way through film school. Her earnings had financed the start of the public relations business that had led him to the technology company he'd just sold.

Mom had never quite recovered from the discovery of my dad's affair. She'd gotten heavier, hadn't dated. But still she worked. Full-time. Day in, day out.

"She'll be taken care of," Dad said. "This was contemplated in the divorce agreement."

The way he said it made me suspicious. I let the thought pass. "Congratulations again, Dad," I said. We said our good-byes and hung up.

I lay back on the couch and thought about how our family had struggled with money all my life. I was happy for my father, but part of me felt like I'd been cheated. Now that he could finally take care of me in the way I'd always wanted, I no longer needed it.

A year had passed. I was loving the life of a Wall Street trader. Every day, I woke at 5:15 a.m., took a cab to the Midtown trading floor of Bank of America, sat down at my desk, and didn't get up for twelve hours except to go to the bathroom. At night I went to dinners or ball games with clients. I didn't enjoy the dinners, but I liked that I was important enough to be invited; every client wanted to meet the telecom trader. When I got home, I'd dive into bed so I could get a few hours of sleep before doing it all again.

I was twenty-five, and now I had an intern sitting next to me, asking *me* questions. In the year since I'd been back in New York, I had discovered some of the perks of being a Wall Street trader. Her name was Katie.

I met Katie a few weeks after the Verizon new issue. One hot-winded New York summer night, I was riding home in a cab after another client dinner. The window was down and the warm air brushed over my face. I wasn't ready to go home, so I called Lance Peters.

Lance Peters was a bond broker, which meant he facilitated trades between traders at investment banks. I was one of his clients. I did not like Lance. He was one of those guys born on third base, convinced he'd hit a triple. But I knew he'd be out on the town, and I wanted company.

He was at Hudson Bar and Books, a block from my apartment, sitting at an outdoor table with a pencil-thin blonde in a summer dress. Lance introduced us. When I ordered a Diet Coke and she didn't comment, I knew Lance had told her I was sober. I was grateful I had reached a position where I didn't always have to explain myself; now, sometimes, other people did it for me.

When Lance suggested we grab a nightcap at the Gansevoort hotel in the Meatpacking District, I agreed. Normally, I would've gone home to bed, but Katie had laughed at some of my jokes and I thought I had a chance. I was excited—I hadn't had a woman interested in me since Sloane Taylor. The years in Charlotte were dry and lonely.

At the Gansevoort hotel, we met a bunch of Lance's friends. When Katie said hello to them and then turned back toward me, her dress whipping tight against her body, I knew she was interested. At midnight I walked her to a cab. She declined my invitation to see my apartment, but when the cab pulled up, she leaned in and kissed me on the mouth, and then ducked into the backseat.

Our first date was at a French restaurant in the Meatpacking District, and while I waited for Katie to arrive, I thought delightedly about what I'd learned about her. Jack, a trader I worked with, had gone to high school with her and said her nickname had been Regina George, after the popular girl played by Rachel McAdams in *Mean Girls*. Katie was the recipient of the Class Body award (*They really have that?* I'd asked), and Jack was impressed I was taking her out.

Katie arrived for our date looking tan and sexy. When the waiter seated us, I noticed she looked nervous. I could guess why.

"Don't mind me," I said. "Drink whatever you want."

"Thank God," she blurted out. "First dates can be so awkward."

She ordered wine. When it came, she held the glass lightly at the ends of her long manicured fingers. I was glad she was drinking. I still felt uncool not drinking, so I enjoyed having some wine on the table, although I made sure to keep my nose away from it, because the heady smell of merlot made me salivate. Also, Katie getting tipsy took some pressure off me to make interesting conversation; the more she drank, the more easily she laughed.

We went home together that night, and many nights after, and soon I had a girlfriend.

Katie loved nice restaurants and I loved being seen with her, so we went out a lot. On summer weekends, Katie and I would drive out to Westhampton where her family kept a small apartment. We went to the beach during the day—she read *US Weekly*; I read *Barron's*—and at night we went out for fresh seafood.

I took Katie on a Caribbean vacation. The resort in Turks and Caicos, Parrot Cay, cost $600 a night. I learned how to windsurf, we had sex in the afternoons, and we ate too much at every meal. After spending our third afternoon at the beach, we returned to our room. Instead of having sex, we each picked up our books. Lying on that pillow-top bed, in my fresh terry-cloth robe, with the ocean breeze wafting in through the window, next to my beautiful, blond girlfriend, I realized I was bored. For a moment it seemed like Katie and I were just actors, playing the role of a happy couple.

Still, I loved that I was dating Katie. I loved how she looked on my arm. I loved our life, the expensive restaurants, the island vacations, the apartment in the Hamptons. So it didn't bother me that sometimes I didn't like her.

She was an unflinching gossip. Sometimes listening to her eviscerate someone behind their back, I felt ill. She urged her best friend to dump a guy because he was a penniless writer (who now writes for the *New Yorker* and *Vanity Fair*). She also didn't like to talk about relationship problems; if we had an argument, she preferred to just forget it.

But the real problem with Katie was that she was not Sloane Taylor.

One day, Sloane called and asked if I was free for dinner in New York. I had dreamed about her the night before, in bed next to Katie. In my dream Sloane was getting married, and I was flying to LA to stop the wedding.

It was supposed to be a dinner between friends, but I spent weeks researching the perfect restaurant. I finally secured a table at Bette, a new spot started by the owner of Bungalow 8, the hippest club in New York. Bette was perfect—dark, candlelit, trendy but intimate.

When she walked in, I felt leveled by her beauty. We sat down, ordered, and started talking about old times. When our conversation led us to the time we saw *Les Misérables* together, I asked Sloane to sing the song we both loved. She was bashful about her voice, and I thought she'd say no, but she didn't. I leaned forward in the quiet stillness of our dark table and listened as, almost in a whisper, she began to sing.

> There is a castle on a cloud.
> I like to go there in my sleep.

The song is about a fantasy, and as Sloane's lovely voice traced quietly over the beautiful words, it was as if I heard them for the first time. I heard the sorrow and sadness of Cosette's words, the words of a young girl clinging to the life she has created in her mind to distract her from the pain of her reality. Something nagged in my consciousness, as if this time, the song pertained to me, but I dismissed that and instead stared with huge eyes at the woman I loved, who was not the woman I was dating. If Sloane had asked me to get back together at that moment, I would have said yes. She didn't.

CHAPTER 27

A Handwritten Note

◻

In the summer of 2006, at the age of twenty-six, I flew home for my sister's high school graduation. I was nervous. I planned to confront my father. A year had passed since he became a millionaire, and I'd finally learned how much of his windfall my mother received.

Years earlier, when they were negotiating the divorce agreement, my mom was spending most of her days in bed, still crushed by the revelation of my father's affair. She hired a bumpkin of a lawyer; Dad hired a shark. His lawyer inserted a clause that stipulated, in the event my father's company sold, the proceeds would be split according to a complex calculation. Mom didn't realize that the calculation diminished her share over time. When the technology company finally sold, three years after the divorce, they applied the calculation. The result: Dad, 90 percent; Mom, 10 percent.

I was far from my mother's champion, but even I knew that calculus wasn't fair. I'd watched my mom slave overtime for years. I couldn't believe Dad would allow her to keep working, while he and Sara took early retirement. I kept expecting to hear that he had increased her share, but he didn't. After a few months, I brought up the subject with him.

"That's between your mother and me," he said.

But I felt like it impacted our whole family. And it wasn't just how he was treating Mom. It was how he was treating everyone.

When Bain transferred Ben to London, Dad offered to accompany him during the move to help him find an apartment. Ben, whose bank account was near empty, was thrilled. Now that Dad was a millionaire, Ben thought he might help furnish his new apartment. But when Ben asked for money, Dad got furious. Ben started crying. Dad said, "Your tears mean nothing to me." He caught a cab to the airport and boarded the next plane home. Ben called me, burst into tears, and asked me to wire him money so he could eat dinner that night.

Dad had always been tightfisted. In high school he insisted Ben and I share a drivers license—we looked so much alike that a cop would never be able to tell the difference—so that we would only have to pay for one car insurance policy. In college Ben had gotten a DUI on my license. I'd always thought Dad was cheap because he didn't have enough money. As a millionaire, he seemed more miserly than ever.

The consequences of living with a father whose focus was entirely on his new money and new wife, and with a mother still shattered from divorce, were apparent in the waistlines and addictive habits of my younger brother and sister. Julia was nearing two hundred pounds and had gotten in several fistfights at school. Daniel had graduated from pot to cocaine, from obese to morbidly obese. He spent a lot of time on the streets and usually wouldn't arrive at Dad's downtown apartment until well after midnight.

I was worried about Daniel and Julia, and was pissed about how Dad seemed to be hoarding money, even from his own family. Since Dad wouldn't answer the questions I asked about Mom, I started asking him questions that pertained to me. What, I asked him, is in your will? I wanted to know how much my siblings and I would get, and how much his new wife would get. At first, he wouldn't talk about it. But I persisted until he agreed to discuss the matter.

We sat across from each other at a coffee shop. He said that in the event of his death, Sara would get half the money. The other half would be for my siblings and me. I was angry that Sara would get more than my mom, or me. Then Dad told me that there were conditions on my inheritance. Upon his death, the money would be put in a trust. Instead of getting a lump sum, each of the children would get a monthly stipend. If we wanted a large amount, for a down payment on a house or to start a business, we would have to apply to the trust. He called it the "I Have a Dream" clause. He looked pleased with himself.

"Who decides if our application is approved?" I asked.

"Sara, of course," he said. "She'll control the trust."

I sat silently as I let the reality of his words sink in. If I wanted my inheritance, I'd have to ask permission from the woman who'd broken up our family. I was so frustrated.

"Dad," I spluttered, near tears. "My *job* is managing money. I'm sober. I'm successful. I'm doing everything right. Why don't you trust . . ."

Suddenly I stopped. I closed my mouth and just looked at him. *What was I doing?* Here I was, still trying to earn my father's trust, when it was he who should have been trying to earn mine.

I leaned back in my chair and regarded him. He was leaning forward, tensed, ready to engage. He was always ready to argue, to explain why he was right. We'd done a few joint sessions with Linda over the past year, and no matter what I said, Dad had a retort, a justification, an explanation of why I was wrong. I'd also had sessions with Mom, and she'd tearfully apologized, for hitting me, for being late, for being checked out during my childhood. Not Dad. He could never be accountable. He could never apologize.

I was tired of this. I thought about that time in the car with Marshall Masters. *A hundred thousand dollars*, Marshall had said. *No questions asked. I trust you.* It had been so easy for Marshall to trust me and treat me with respect. For Dad, it was impossible.

What I really wanted from Dad wasn't money. In college I'd watched my friend Francisco, who came from a poorer family than mine, receive care packages in the mail. His parents would send underwear, socks, and whatever money they could scrape together. Sometimes it was only twenty bucks in crumpled singles. But there was always a handwritten note telling Francisco how much they loved him.

Dad never did anything like that.

I was tired of him. I didn't need money, especially money with conditions. I did need love from him, but I was never going to get that. Not because something was wrong with me, but because something was wrong with him.

I stood up from the table, looked down at him, and finally uttered the words I had held on to for years but had been unable to say.

"Fuck you, Dad," I said.

And I walked out.

CHAPTER 28

The Navy SEALs of Bond Trading

◻

In the spring of 2007, my star was rising on Wall Street. Alexei and I and one of our colleagues had invented a new type of CDS contract based on a complex subsidiary spin-off transaction, which put me at the vanguard of CDS market innovation. In the first few months of the year, a huge position I'd taken in the bonds and CDSs of Alltel Corporation suddenly doubled in value, and I was already up $8 million in profit.

My success at work wasn't just professional. It was social, too. I'd become close with the other traders. I felt like I belonged. Like a leader, even. A boxing class I organized had become a huge success. Every morning at 4:45 a.m. twenty traders met at a boxing gym. We'd wrap our hands, pound the heavy bag, and work one-on-one in the ring with private trainers. I loved it. It wasn't that I enjoyed the boxing, which I didn't, or waking up that early, which I certainly didn't. I loved that people showed up to something I spearheaded. I'd been waiting my whole life to have that kind of pull.

Ben and my five-year anniversary of getting sober was approaching. "Isn't it crazy how far we've come?" I asked during one of our daily calls. Ben had been the first person in his class to be promoted at Bain and had recently been accepted into Harvard's John F. Kennedy School of Government. He'd realized he'd rather spend his life working to help the less fortunate than making money. When Ben got into Harvard, I felt happy for him. For the first time, I didn't feel jealous of his success.

"It's amazing how much can happen in five years," he said.

Katie and I had moved into a giant, $6,000-per-month loft apartment on Bond Street, with twenty-foot ceilings and floor-to-ceiling windows. To get a better deal, I paid the entire year's rent—$72,000—up front. I didn't think twice about writing a check that size, because a month earlier, Alexei and Marshall had pulled me into a room and told me my bonus for the prior year was $500,000.

A few weeks later, I received a phone call that made even that $500,000 look like chump change. The head of corporate trading at Citibank called and offered me a guaranteed $1.75 million per year for two years to trade telecom for Citibank.

That would permanently establish me in a higher compensation bracket. Wall Street traders like to say their jobs are risky; they aren't. Once you are paid a certain amount, you rarely drop far below that, even in a down year. When I was offered $1.75 million for two years after just three and a half years on Wall Street, I knew I was going to become a rich man.

But I didn't just want to be very rich. I wanted to be *super* rich. While the Citibank job would make me a millionaire, it wouldn't make me a billionaire.

In bond and CDS trading, there is a strict hierarchy. At the bottom are investment-grade traders (which is what I was), who traffic in the bonds and CDSs of the safest, least volatile companies. On the next rung up are high-yield traders, who trade the volatile bonds and CDSs of lower-rated corporations. At the top of the pyramid is an elite class of traders, who traffic in the bonds and CDSs of companies in or near bankruptcy. They are called distressed traders.

Distressed traders are the Navy SEALs of bond trading. Their job requires deep intellect and balls of steel. They need the brainpower to interpret balance sheets and understand complex covenants in loan documents, and the fortitude to withstand volatility that exists nowhere else in the markets. Prices of distressed bonds can double or halve in a single day. Of all the traders at investment banks like Goldman Sachs or Morgan Stanley, distressed traders make the most money. Many leave to start hedge funds, and become billionaires.

By the time Citibank offered me a "1.75 by 2," I'd already set my mind on bigger things. It was like the moment in *The Social Network* where Justin Timberlake says, "A million dollars isn't cool. You know what's cool? A billion dollars."

I told Marshall about Citibank's offer and that I wanted to use the offer to negotiate a move to the distressed desk at B of A. Marshall said he would help. At first the head of the distressed desk wasn't interested, but Marshall not only convinced him that my CDS expertise would help them in the upcoming bankruptcy cycle, but also agreed to pay half of my bonus that year out of the investment-grade bonus pool. It was a stunningly generous move, especially by Wall Street standards. I may not have been born with a good father, but I had found one.

I became the youngest distressed trader at Bank of America.

I thought I'd finally made it. But in June, when I was invited by a CDS broker to Las Vegas with a bunch of other traders and our girlfriends to watch the Mayweather–De La Hoya fight, my worldview began to change.

I'd never been in a chopper before. A Lincoln Town Car picked Katie and me up from Bank of America and drove us to a helipad downtown, where we met the other traders and boarded a helicopter to take us to the airport. As we lifted off, the helicopter swayed from side to side. When our flight arrived in Vegas, we took a limo to the Hard Rock. The CDS broker who had arranged the trip handed me keys to our room and told us to meet him at the restaurant in the basement of the hotel.

Brokers are at the bottom of the Wall Street power structure. They earn money by facilitating trades between traders at investment banks. Traders at investment banks earn money by facilitating trades between "clients" (insurance companies, hedge funds, money managers). Brokers' livelihoods depend on keeping traders happy, so you can say anything to them. If you told a broker that you'd just slept with his mother, he'd probably respond, "Nice one!"

Entertaining is such a huge part of Wall Street—traders take out clients, and brokers take out traders—because if a dinner, strip club, or all-expenses-paid vacation might result in a trade, then nothing is too expensive. A broker might earn $10,000 on a single trade, so unless the night costs more than $10,000, it's worth it. And if the night costs more, well, there are many trades to be done.

I remember how powerful I felt when I realized I could go to any restaurant in Manhattan—Per Se, Le Bernardin—just by picking up the phone. I could go to whatever ball game I wanted—Yankees/Red Sox, Knicks/Lakers, the World Series—just by hinting to a broker that I might be interested. If I accepted an invitation, it was as if I were doing *them* a favor. One broker gave me their car-service account number. When I flew in from out of town, a sleek, black Lincoln Town Car waited for me at the airport.

It wasn't about the money. I could have afforded all of this myself. It was about the power. Because of how smart and successful I was, it was someone else's *job* to make me happy. I didn't even like going out with brokers. Wall Street dinners usually consisted of talking about which traders were losing money, talking about the waitress's ass, and making fun of each other's clothes—*Nice shirt, douche bag!* But I liked that I could.

The restaurant in the bottom of the hotel was the new Las Vegas branch of the famed New York sushi restaurant Nobu. I knew the signature Nobu meal by heart—yellowtail jalapeño sashimi, rock shrimp tempura, Kobe beef medallions you could cut with the edge of your fork, a huge plate of delicate sushi and sashimi, followed by a light dessert of mochi-wrapped ice cream. Dinner at Nobu could cost $500 a person.

After dinner our group of traders and their girlfriends took a limo to Marquee. Marquee was a club with three different velvet-rope lines; you had to be an A-list actor or arrive with a throng of models to get in. When we stepped out of the limo, our CDS broker walked up to a ponytailed Persian man dressed head to toe in white. The Persian man led us to the front of each of the three lines and whispered to the bouncer, who let us pass with a smile. When we got into the club, we were ushered to a private table in the center of the floor. Cocktail waitresses in tight black dresses started bringing out bottles of champagne and vodka.

My eyes left Katie's hips and roamed across the flashing lights and dancing bodies until they finally landed on a six-foot-four, two hundred–pound trader, dancing like a gorilla fifteen feet from me. I knew Jeff—we worked together—and he was obviously drunk. He seemed to be chanting something over and over again. I leaned in closer to see if I could make out the words.

"Thirty-five sticks! I'm up thirty-five sticks!"

Son of a bitch. In trader lingo, a stick equals a million dollars. Jeff was a high-yield trader. He was already up $35 million on the year, compared with my $8 million, and he was pounding his chest and bragging about it. Cold liquid jealousy seeped into my stomach. If the year ended like this, Jeff would get paid more than me.

I had to remind myself that I was on the distressed desk. Ultimately I was in a better position. *Thirty-five million bucks is nothing compared to where I'm going, Jeff.* He didn't realize yet that compared to me, he was already a second-class citizen. I was the only distressed trader on the trip—I had a better shot of making a billion dollars than any of them.

But a memory tugged at me. I remembered the moment when I came across that compensation document that showed how much more money CDS traders earn than bond traders. I'd thought that if only I could become a CDS trader, I'd feel successful. Well, I'd done it. I'd become a CDS trader. And yet, it still wasn't enough. For just a moment, I wondered if becoming a distressed trader would be enough, either.

I called Katie over. She was dancing, and I had to shout to get her attention. When she saw me, she smiled and seductively danced over.

"Are you okay?" she asked. "Having a good time?"

"Yes, yes," I said. "Great time."

"Are you sure?"

"Yeah."

Just then another bottle of Dom Pérignon arrived. I poured myself some club soda. Katie started dancing next to me, and I sat quietly with my thoughts. I wanted to like this more than I did. I wanted to be the kind of person who did stuff like this and enjoyed it. But I was sober, and no matter how cool of a place I was in, I was still sober. The problem with being in a bar when you aren't drunk is that everyone else is.

But it was more than that. There was something hollow about the satisfaction of realizing your life finally matches your fantasy. Instead of feeling complete, I felt sad.

"Hey, let's go," I said to Katie. "I'm tired."

She looked like a kid whose toy had been taken away. "Now?" she asked. "But it's so early!" It was midnight.

"Okay," I said. "Half an hour more?"

"Great!" she said, and kissed me on the cheek. Then she stood up, wobbling, and started dancing next to the table. I steeled myself for another thirty minutes. My nights often ended like this, at dinners or bars, waiting until it was okay for me to go home.

My eyes fastened again on Katie's hips. They were exquisite, but as I watched her I realized they were just hips. I didn't even know who she was. I mean, I could describe her personality—she was smart, fun, had a great sense of humor, and was a huge gossip—but I didn't know what lay beneath. I didn't know what terrified her, what she loved with abandon. Even at home, when we were alone, we never ventured far below the surface.

With ten minutes to go in my self-imposed prison sentence, I took a sweeping look over the grand surroundings: the thumping, flashing club; the successful traders; the beautiful women. I was twenty-seven years old, on the verge of becoming a multimillionaire. I'd made it. I'd *achieved*. My life looked exactly like I'd wanted it to look.

And with a sinking feeling of horror, a question that had been sitting on the periphery of my consciousness stepped forward into the light.

So why am I so miserable?

CHAPTER 29

The Anniversary Presents

◻

On the morning of Inauguration Day at the White House, the president and the president elect have coffee together and then leave for the inauguration ceremony. Then, all hell breaks loose. The White House staff has six hours to pack the old president's furniture and belongings, clean, then move in the new president. For privacy reasons, no outside staffers are hired. There are only two elevators. For six hours the White House is in chaos, a flurry of frantic activity. It's a changing of the guard.

Sometimes, the same thing can happen inside a person.

Two months after Vegas, my five-year sober anniversary and my two-year anniversary with Katie fell on the same weekend. I was concerned that Katie wouldn't like her anniversary present.

I had set the bar high. Over the years I had bought her $700 Christian Louboutin high heels, a thousand-dollar ring from Bulgari, and spent tens of thousands on restaurants and vacations.

But for our two-year anniversary, I wanted to do something special. The first thing I bought was a bag she had admired in Bergdorf Goodman that cost $3,000. I didn't like the idea of a $3,000 bag, but she liked it, so I figured, *What the hell?*

When I got home, I took the bag out of the box and wondered, *Is this enough?* I played through a scenario in my head where I handed her the bag, and she said thank you, but inside she thought, *Is this it?* I remembered she once mentioned her friend raving about a five-star French restaurant called Daniel. I made a reservation.

But something still gnawed at me. I wanted her to be blown away. I remembered hearing a friend of Katie's talk about an anniversary where she and her husband had spent the weekend at the Mandarin Oriental on Central Park. It was only a few blocks from their apartment, but she said it had felt like a minivacation. They had stayed in and ordered room service and gotten massages all weekend.

"It was like we were hiding from our real lives," she said.

I booked a room at a similarly expensive hotel, the Palace.

The night of our anniversary, when we walked into the room at the Palace, I knew immediately that I had made a mistake. Katie was trendy; the room was old and frilly, like it was designed for grandparents or British people. She smiled when I told her we had dinner reservations at Daniel. But when I brought out the gift-wrapped box from Bergdorf's, her face fell. I knew suddenly that instead of too little, it was all too much.

"But I didn't get you a present," she protested.

"Don't worry," I said. "Just open this."

She opened it and smiled and kissed me. Her lips were trembling. I smiled, trying to show her it didn't bother me that she hadn't gotten me anything.

We went to Daniel. The dining room reminded me of Versailles. Intimidated by the career waiter in a tuxedo, I stumbled through my order. Six waiters hovered near our table; I found myself whispering to Katie so they wouldn't hear our conversation. When we came back to the room, we had sex, because it seemed like we were supposed to. In the morning, we checked out early.

As we walked outside, I asked what her plans were for the day.

"I'm going to brunch with the girls," she said. It was her turn to see my face fall.

"What's wrong?" she asked.

I paused, realizing that she didn't know.

"Today is my five-year anniversary," I said. "Five years sober."

"Oh no," she said. "You never told me. Do you want me to cancel?"

I put my hands up. "No, no, no," I said. I kissed her, put her in a cab, and then walked down Fifth Avenue.

If you'd seen me walking down the street that day, you might have thought I was crazy. My face contorted, I kept running my right hand through my hair, and I was carrying on a running conversation with myself.

At first I thought I was pissed at Katie.

Why hadn't she remembered? Why hadn't she gotten me anything? But then, as I thought about it, I realized I wasn't angry at her.

I was angry at myself.

I hadn't even told Katie it was my five-year anniversary. Sobriety was one of the things I was most proud of in my life. It was at the core of who I'd become. It was the glue that reconnected Ben and me. So why hadn't I told my live-in girlfriend about it? Why was I hiding myself from her?

And why had I gone so over-the-top with my presents? *Is it enough?* I'd wondered. I had to make sure the presents were enough. Had to make sure that *the presents* would impress her.

I stopped walking. *Is it enough?* What I'd really been asking was, *Am I enough?* And the answer? No. I am not enough. My core belief. That's what the presents were about. That's why I'd hid myself from Katie. That's why I always needed more money, a bigger job, a better-looking girl on my arm.

I was compensating, because at heart I didn't believe I was enough.

I thought about our apartment. It was enormous. We had needed to buy a second living room set, because just one couch looked too small in the massive space. Now we had two sitting areas. Why would two people need two separate sitting areas?

I stood on Fifth Avenue, across from Rockefeller Plaza, and felt something emerge from beneath the confines of my mind. From beneath the ego and the arrogance. It looked around at the pretty frivolity of my life, and it said, I want *more*. And I knew it was talking about something completely different than the *more* I had tried to buy, to earn.

I walked all the way home from the Palace in Midtown to my Bond Street apartment in the Village. By the time I arrived, I'd reached a decision. The apartment seemed cavernous as I sat on the couch and called Linda.

"What's going on?" she asked.

I told her about Katie and the presents. "I want a different kind of life," I said.

"Ah," she said. "You found your heart." Years later she told me she'd been waiting a long time for that call, for me to start owning who I was becoming.

That night, I lay next to Katie in our big bed. She had come home, we had made up, and she had fallen asleep an hour ago. But I was a thousand miles from sleep.

I was thinking about what happened eight years earlier, when I'd gone over the top with Sloane's presents on Valentine's day—two dozen roses, Broadway tickets, fresh lobster. I'd thought I'd done that because I was so in love. But now I saw that the presents for Sloane were exactly the same as the presents for Katie. What I'd thought was love was just using someone to make me feel important.

I would never have called myself a misogynist, but that night, lying in bed, I saw that I'd mistreated women my whole life. In some way, I was doing the same thing to Katie that Dad had done to Mom. I was staying with her even though I didn't love her. I was wasting her time, because I didn't have the backbone to tell her the truth.

Just like Dad.

I called my mom that weekend, just to say hi. As I listened to her talk, my heart filled with sadness. Not just about what her life was like now—she was old, lonely, and overweight from years of stuffing down her pain with secret bowls of vanilla ice cream—but about what her life had been.

She had been abused her whole life. Her alcoholic father and crazy-eyed mother had waged emotional warfare on her and her sisters, and Mom, as the oldest, bore the brunt of it.

She ran away from home at seventeen and fell in love, but her fiancé hung himself in the trailer they shared. After that she lost any hope for a different life and went back to what she knew. She married my dad, who hit her in the beginning, then commenced an even more insidious attack, enlisting her children as enemy soldiers.

I had become one of those enemy soldiers. I'd watched Dad fling poisonous darts at my mom since I was a kid. Soon I was hurling my own darts at my mother. My brothers and sister all followed. Mom was a scapegoat in the family she'd been born into, and a scapegoat in the one she built herself.

All the good memories came rushing back. How she taught me to swim in a hotel pool by promising me a banana split if I reached the other side. The times she, Ben, and I danced in the gardens on the Navajo reservation we'd lived on when I was four, praying for rain. How, at Six Flags Magic Mountain, she'd leave us in line for one roller coaster to save our place in the next line. The time I pointed with five-year-old fingers to the mountain range in the distance and told her I was going to walk there, and she smiled and walked with me until I tired.

It wasn't that I forgot the damaging things she had done.

But in that moment I forgave her. I knew that she'd loved me as best she could.

Then I thought about how I'd mistreated Sloane and Katie. I saw that a whole lifetime of watching my father treat my mother with disdain had taught me to view *all* women with disdain. I became aware of all of the wonderful women who had come into my life. Elyn Walker, who'd shown me how to get sober. Sloane Taylor, who'd brought me into counseling and shown me that even cool people get help. And, of course, Linda. They were real-life refutations to the story my father put in my head.

The dam broke. Seeing the destruction my dad had caused my mom, I started to face the damage I'd caused the women in my life. I decided to begin repairs.

CHAPTER 30

Sacred Creatures

○

Katie and I started couples counseling. The counselor was a diminutive, academic-looking woman with cropped gray hair and big glasses. As soon as we sat down in front of her, Katie started crying. When the counselor asked if she knew why she was upset, Katie said no. For the entire session, tears that she could not explain poured down her cheeks. We went a few times, but we hadn't gotten very far. We were still living together in our sepulcher of an apartment, a crypt for the living death of our relationship.

I knew I needed to make amends with my mother. I flew out to Seattle to help her sell a condo she'd purchased and reorganize her finances. I offered to find an attorney for her to seek recourse for the divorce. I collected all the documents and then started calling divorce lawyers in Seattle. Some wouldn't speak to me after hearing who my father's attorney was. I finally connected with one of the top divorce attorneys in Seattle who spoke in rapid, clipped bursts. He asked why it'd taken me so long to look into this. I told him I'd only recently discovered how much help my mom needed.

"That's unfortunate," he said. "Over three years have passed, making it very unlikely we could get a judge to overturn."

Mom didn't seem surprised. It was as if she'd accepted that my father would always beat her. But I could hear in her voice that she was grateful someone had taken her side.

When I returned home, I knew things with Katie had to end. During a counseling session I told Katie it was over. She begged me to give it a few months, and the counselor suggested I do the same, but I couldn't. I knew I didn't love her. She moved out one weekend when I was away. When I returned home, the apartment was half empty. I walked through the cavernous space, my footsteps echoing off the twenty-foot-high ceilings, and thought about the brand-name life I finally had but no longer wanted. I had six months remaining on the year's rent I paid in advance, but I decided to move into a tiny apartment in Alphabet City that fit me better.

After that, I felt better about the direction of my life. But something nagged at me. There was still something that my father had taught me—something big—that continued to impact how I treated women.

It started when I was twelve. I found a tattered porn magazine in the bottom drawer of my dad's bedside table. I took the magazine and hid it under the couch in the living room. When the house was asleep, I crept out of bed and retrieved it. Wide-eyed, I read the erotic stories and masturbated for the first time. It was, to that point, the greatest moment of my life.

My dad unknowingly provided me with a steady supply of smutty magazines and books, and I was perpetually sneaking them from his drawers. In high school, I started to buy porn magazines myself from shady-looking liquor stores. The cashier would put them in a brown shame bag, and I'd slide the bag into the back waist of my jeans before walking out. I looked at porn for five years before I even had sex. By the time I lost my virginity, almost everything I knew about sex came from porn.

In college, I no longer had to endure the shame of buying magazines from a person, or even buying anything at all.

Columbia had broadband Internet access. Always a reader, I preferred stories to pictures or videos. There were millions of stories online, available for free.

As an adult, looking at or reading porn became a regular part of my life. When I found myself alone at home, I'd open the computer or turn on one of the soft-core flicks on Cinemax. The amount I watched or read ebbed and flowed—sometimes daily, sometimes once a week, depending largely on whether I had a girlfriend or not. I didn't become obsessed; porn didn't take over my life. Instead, it was one of those enjoyable life habits that I always looked forward to, like morning coffee.

At the same time, I knew it wasn't innocuous. I knew because I was ashamed. I never spoke about it. I would make sure the doors were double-locked, the shades drawn. I deleted the history on my computers and was nervous whenever anyone picked up my cable remote control in case they might click the Recently Viewed button. After getting sober, I'd cut out everything in my life that I was ashamed about, except for expensive haircuts and pornography.

The fact was that I needed it. Sometimes I would try to masturbate without pornography. And it would happen, the process would happen. But it wouldn't be the same. It would take longer, and be less charged. It lacked the rush. The excitement. The drug.

Around that time, I came across an article about how a large percentage of porn actresses were sexually abused as kids. That hit me in the gut. I knew from experience that how you were treated as a child impacted your behavior as an adult.

It made sense to me that girls who'd been sexually abused were more likely to go into a sexual profession. They had learned at an early age that their bodies were for the use of men—that the only places they would get real attention was on their backs or their knees. I had learned from my dad that money would make me safe and important, and had made my way to a Wall Street trading desk. They had learned from their dads, or their uncles or neighbors or family friends, that sex made them valuable, worthy of attention, and made their way to dark street corners, stripper poles, or video cameras that could stream to the Internet.

I talked to some guys about the article, and they said they thought porn or stripping was a good trade: a woman can put herself through college working far less than she would as a waitress. But I questioned the fairness of that trade.

Despite what I was learning, I continued to use porn. I figured the videos had already been made; I was just watching them. The porn industry was going to exist whether or not I participated in it.

But soon I realized that my logic was flawed. I was part of the demand. Maybe my viewing one Cinemax film was the tipping point that caused the production of another. Maybe my viewership was responsible for the humiliation of that woman, naked on her knees in front of twenty people on set, and millions of eyes through the Internet.

But it wasn't just about porn actresses—it was about what the proliferation of porn meant for all women. I was amazed, as I looked into the statistics, at the sheer amount of sexual violence in our culture. Almost half of all women are raped or face attempted rape; 38 percent of girls are sexually molested. Porn is an integral part of a misogynist culture that makes it difficult and dangerous to be a woman in America.

I understood this reality because I had begun to notice how porn changed the way I looked at women. There's a scarcity of women on trading floors, and the few who are there are often in assistant roles. Because of this scarcity and subordination, there's an oft-used term—"trading-floor hot"—which means that a woman you ordinarily wouldn't look twice at in regular life seems attractive at work. Not attractive in that you'd want to marry them, but attractive in that you'd like to fuck them.

A woman walking down a trading row might turn around to see half of the traders she passed leaning back in their chairs ogling her. The more porn I looked at, the more overpowering my trading floor fantasies became.

Porn wasn't just teaching me how to treat some women; it was teaching me how to treat *all* women. That's when I realized that porn wasn't about sex—it was about power. Porn was teaching me that women were there to be used by me, whenever I wanted. I had thought porn was about sex and arousal, but now I saw it was about denigration.

So I quit. A few months after Katie and I broke up I disconnected Cinemax and pledged not to read another story or look at another picture. At first it was hard. I'd come home from work and just want the release I knew porn would give me. But I didn't open the computer. Days turned into weeks, and after a while the urges began to subside.

One night, I went out to dinner with a managing director and a high-profile client to a churrascaria—a Brazilian all-you-can-eat meat buffet—on Fifty-Fourth and Eighth Avenue. The MD and the client were old friends, and they rapidly got red-faced drunk. About an hour in, the waitress swung by to ask if they'd like another round—two Glenlivets. As she walked away, they both stared hard at her ass. The client turned to me and said, "I'd like to bend her over the table, give her some meat." The managing director roared.

"What's wrong, Sam?" said the client, noticing I wasn't laughing. I forced a smile, and said "Nothing." The managing director ordered another round.

In the cab home, I was furious. I should have spoken up, but I hadn't.

CHAPTER 31

Gatsby, Interrupted

A few months after I started on the distressed desk at Bank of America, the market fell off a cliff. This was great for me. I'd been bearish and very vocal about it. I'd constructed a portfolio of complex trades that would, I thought, profit in a market collapse. As the market began to plummet, my reputation skyrocketed. I was invited into meetings way above my pay grade, with Marshall, the head of distressed, and even the head of the investment bank. When my facility with derivatives became apparent, the head of the investment bank asked me to meet with the heads of all the business lines, to assess their derivatives risk. I was a young trader, but all of a sudden I was meeting one-on-one with the head of equities, the head of mortgages, the head of treasuries.

That was the apex of my career at Bank of America.

It turned out that I had overlooked an important variable when I'd constructed my portfolio—the difference between how bonds and derivatives perform in a funding crisis. I owned a lot of bonds and had shorted derivatives against them. I'd thought the spread between them would compress; instead, the bonds started to plummet, while the derivatives stayed put. I lost $5 million the first week, $5 million the second week, and then $10 million the third week. Soon there were rumors I'd be fired.

Marshall was losing money, too. He'd seen the crash coming and put on a massive short position. But his bosses disagreed with his call and forced him to exit the trade. A week later the market plummeted. Without his short position as a hedge, the desk he ran started losing money. Marshall was blamed for the losses.

On Wall Street your reputation can change by the day. That's how it was for both Marshall and me. One week we were on top of the world. The next week we were on the verge of getting fired.

I loved Marshall more than ever. I'd heard that he'd stood up for me in a management meeting where my losses were being discussed, even though his own job was in jeopardy.

One day, when yet another market drop left both our portfolios bloody, I typed a Bloomberg message—the instant messaging system traders use to communicate with each other—to Marshall:

The train is heading for the cliff

His response came almost immediately.

And the doors are double-locked

I chuckled and then wrote back.

And it's on fire

In the midst of misery, we shared a laugh. While Marshall's laugh was hearty, mine was grudging. Sitting at my desk watching my portfolio bleed, I felt like I couldn't breathe. Like I was drowning.

That's when Sean Mallory, the head of trading at Pateras, called me. I told Marshall immediately, and he said I couldn't have dreamt up a more perfect job. Pateras offered me a million dollars, and I accepted. A week later I resigned from Bank of America. Marshall walked with me over to Pateras. I hugged him and thanked him for all that he'd done for my career. Then I walked in and signed my contract.

A few weeks later, Marshall was fired. An article was written about it in the *New York Post*.

Six months later, I rented two houses on Fire Island and invited Mom, my siblings, and two close friends out for a family vacation.

Fire Island is just an hour train ride and a twenty-minute ferry outside New York, but it's a different world. The island is only a half mile wide, and there are no cars because there are no roads. Wood-planked paths run between houses and up to the sandy beach, and to get somewhere you bike or walk. There are a couple restaurants; mostly you cook for yourself. It's sort of like camping, but in nice houses.

Because it's just an hour outside of New York, it's expensive. But I could afford it. With that year's bonus, I had officially become a millionaire. But unlike my other bonuses, this year I knew that there was nothing I really wanted to buy. Instead, I thought of other ways my money might be useful. I donated a thousand dollars to a congresswoman. I gave $40,000 to charity.

The two houses I rented were cozy, rustic, and stood next to each other, fifty feet from the roaring waves. The first night, we cooked a steak dinner together. When we all sat down at the patio tables, I felt the awesome power of the internal work I'd done. The changes I'd made in my life had begotten changes in my family. Both Ben and my younger brother Daniel were sober, and all my siblings were in counseling with Linda. Mom had almost not come because she was scared, but

I had called and told her I loved her and wanted her there. My siblings had done the same. We all now made efforts to honor her role as the mother of our family. I looked at the excited faces of my brothers, my sister, and my friends, and the fearful, tentative face of my mom, who wasn't used to being included, and I felt how much I was loved and how much I loved in return. I opened my mouth to speak, but I was so overwhelmed that I could barely get any words out. I mumbled something about letting the food get cold and then reached for the steak.

That night I walked alone on the beach. I was feeling my dad's absence. We hadn't spoken in two years, ever since I'd told him to fuck off. I missed him every day, but I was also very angry. Memories of things he'd done swooped through my head like battle hawks. My mind was polluted with them, thousands of instances where Dad had not been what I wanted him to be. So much of my life had been a reaction to my father. I was sick of living in the past, tired of being angry.

Linda had been encouraging me to do a shame ceremony, a Native American practice in which people dug holes in the earth, screamed their rage and shame into those holes, and then covered them, praying for the earth to keep their poisonous emotions.

To me, it just sounded corny. But when I returned from my walk on the beach, I was warming to the idea. I knew I needed to do something to get Dad out of my head.

The kitchen was dark. Daniel was standing by the counter, holding a thick peanut-butter sandwich. Not even an hour had passed since dinner. He looked embarrassed.

Daniel weighed over four hundred pounds. Of all the kids in my family, Daniel had taken the most abuse. He wasn't successful in school like Ben and me, and his failures had infuriated my father. When Daniel was still in elementary school, he'd shown Dad a poor report card in the car. Still driving, Dad clubbed Daniel in the stomach with his fist, and called him an idiot. Dad's rage had been too much for Daniel's tiny body. Now his body had swollen to a size that could accommodate the burden he'd been given to carry.

I understood what Daniel was doing, because I had done something similar myself. That's what my bulimia had been about. I was hungry, not for food, but for love. In college when I'd go to JJ's Place and gorge, I'd feel disgusting afterward, like I didn't deserve all that food, didn't deserve all that love. So I'd eject it from my body.

My brothers and sister had all dealt with our pain differently, but it came from the same place. If you are treated as worthless enough times, you start to believe you deserve it. Then you create an external reality that reflects that.

When I saw that peanut-butter sandwich, I decided, corny or not, we were doing this shame ceremony. I walked over to Daniel and said, "You don't need to hide that from me. I'm your brother. And we are both going to let go of our shame."

On our last morning on Fire Island, my brothers, sister, and I woke before dawn and biked to a secluded beach. We sat in a circle. I explained the process.

We each began to dig a hole in the sand with our hands. There was a sense of embarrassment, but as we reached the tight-packed lower layer of sand, we had to really work, and the embarrassment faded. When our holes were finished, we leaned over and began to whisper into the holes everything we'd ever been ashamed of.

I poured everything into that hole—all the humiliations and embarrassments of my life.

When I finished, I looked up. Julia was crying. Daniel looked like he could talk into his hole forever. Then I heard a deep guttural groan emanate from Ben—it looked as if he were vomiting every humiliation, every failure into that hole. Then he, too, started crying.

They were crying. But I wasn't crying. I'd done enough crying. For me, this ceremony was about saying good-bye. For too long, I had been my father's son. Now my life was about different things—sobriety, healing, love. I was ready to let go of my anger, my sense of injustice.

I thought about the things I was grateful for from Dad— life, shelter, food, college. Dad had done the best he could, and in so many ways I was lucky. I was done being a victim. I would no longer allow how I'd been treated as a boy to control who I was as a man. I was finally ready to take accountability for my life.

Good-bye, Dad. And for the first time since I could remember, I wished him well. I hoped that he was happy and that we would one day talk again.

The last line of *The Great Gatsby* is, "And so we beat on, boats against the current, borne ceaselessly into the past." Well, Jay Gatsby *was* borne ceaselessly into the past. But I had faced my past. Now I was ready to transcend it. For the first time, I looked at the world not through my father's eyes, but through my own.

CHAPTER 32

The Mad Max Scenario

◻

Pateras Capital was founded in 1995 by Eldrick Frost and Peter Conroy, when they were both around my age (twenty-nine). Peter was a distressed trader and Eldrick was a research analyst, and they started Pateras with $4 million. Now, they managed $20 billion. They were both billionaires.

Eldrick and Peter made an unlikely pair. Eldrick had an Ivy League pedigree, and he looked more like a professor than a hedge fund manager. He was bald, save for a few wisps on top, and he wore frumpy sweaters and wrinkled khakis over his soft, pudgy body. He looked like a mole with glasses. But it didn't matter what he looked like; his brain was all that mattered.

People whispered about Eldrick's brain as if it were a national treasure. He was one of those guys you could envision having his brain cryogenically frozen, so that he might bring it back online a hundred years in the future, atop a wheeled robot with a microprocessor heart. It was widely believed he could have cured cancer, or fixed the situation in the Middle East, if only he'd focused on it. But he didn't—he focused on investing, and he was a legend. His job was to know everything about everything, and he did.

Peter was the CEO of the firm and handled the hiring and

firing. He was trim and tan, and his hair looked as if it had been clipped that morning, every day. His ties were worth more than I'd paid in monthly rent down in Charlotte.

And then there was Sean. He was ten years younger than the two managing partners, and not yet a billionaire. But with his talent, intensity, and instincts, he would likely ascend to that esteemed rank.

For the first six months I was there, I loved Pateras. I loved how library-quiet the trading floor was—like a church, but for the worship of money. I loved the freedom I had to focus on any sector, any company. I let my curiosity lead me. Sometimes I'd go into an empty office and read for hours. I couldn't believe I was paid millions to do that. What I loved most of all was how close I got to sit to two billionaires and Sean, the kind of men I'd been reading about my whole life.

But after I returned from Fire Island, things started to look different to me.

If the market crash in 2007 had been a thunderstorm, the 2008 crash was like an earthquake and then a tsunami. In the first quarter of 2008, Countrywide (the largest US mortgage company), Northern Rock (the largest UK finance company), and Bear Stearns (a major US investment bank) all failed.

It's difficult to explain how surreal it was when Bear Stearns went down. Bear Stearns was one of the most prestigious, well-respected institutions on Wall Street; it dissolved over a single week. At the same time, a headline announced that Eliot Spitzer, New York's moralizing governor, was part of a prostitution ring. *Is the world going mad?*

Things got really crazy when Lehman Brothers went down. Lehman was much bigger than Bear Stearns, as powerful as Goldman Sachs, a derivatives behemoth. Because of Lehman's massive derivative exposure, the Lehman bankruptcy roiled the CDS market. Every firm with CDS trades with Lehman suddenly lost all those positions overnight. For the first time in history, there was an emergency derivatives trading session on a Sunday. I received a text that morning from Sean asking me to come to the office. Across Wall Street, trading desks were fully staffed. Billions of dollars' worth of derivatives traded that day.

For the next several months, I worked fourteen-hour days and both days on the weekends. Work was exciting but terrifying. Market dislocations meant opportunity, but now the market wasn't just dislocating; it was disintegrating. I'd come home from work exhausted and fall asleep immediately, waking six hours later, still exhausted.

I was also exhilarated. Almost everyone on Wall Street got killed, except for us. Pateras was positioned defensively, and so we were actually making money during the crash. From a safe vantage, I watched the unmasking of Wall Street. What a rising tide conceals, a falling tide reveals.

I knew the name and biography of every major CEO on Wall Street. I knew the investing style and track record of each manager of the top ten hedge funds. To me, these guys were legends. But in 2008, they all lost money. The average hedge fund was down 20 percent, and almost every investment bank had to be saved from bankruptcy.

It wasn't that I felt superior because I was profitable during the crisis. What bothered me was what the widespread losses said about the nature of the business.

The careers of all these Wall Street legends had spanned one of the greatest bull markets in history. Maybe their returns over that time were less about individual skill and more about the fact that the market had done nothing but go up. Maybe what I'd thought was talent was simply being in the right place at the right time. Wall Street started to look less like a bunch of smartest-guys-in-the-room and more like a group of men who'd secured a seat in a ring of chairs surrounding a huge pile of money, a pile that was growing not because of their skill, but because that's what money did. The system was structured—through monetary policy, carried interest deductions, corporate tax breaks, and industry lobbyists—to ensure it.

That might not sound like a crushing realization, but for me it was. I knew Wall Street wasn't about doing something meaningful with your life, but I had seen it as a great coliseum for my young ambitions. Now it looked less like a meritocracy than an oligarchy.

People were referred to not by their accomplishments but by the size of their bank accounts. People would say, "That guy's worth fifty million dollars," or "That guy has twenty-five million dollars in the bank," without referring to what they had done to earn that money. Because it didn't really matter. Wealth was their only distinguishing feature; guys get rich on Wall Street without doing anything different than the people who came before them.

Near the end of 2008, people started talking about that year's bonuses. Because of the federal bailouts, there was talk about the government limiting bonuses on Wall Street, and many traders were livid.

I empathized with the frustration of traders who'd been profitable that year. They'd made a ton of money for their firms. On the other hand, given that if the government hadn't stepped in they'd be bankrupt, it seemed hard to justify a big bonus. But traders were furious. These were guys whose faces would turn purple talking about the sense of entitlement of union workers who demanded pension payments even when their employers were struggling.

But it was when I heard guys who *lost* money complaining about their bonuses that I started to see the truth about Wall Street. Wall Street wasn't a talent-based meritocracy; it was more like an addiction. Doing whatever you had to do—

rationalizing, lying—to get the money to fill that empty hole inside.

In the spring of 2009 it looked like every financial institution—J.P. Morgan, Citibank, Bank of America—might go down. At Pateras, we often talked about the Mad Max scenario—what life would be like if civilization as we knew it ended. What skill sets would be valued (mechanics, surgeons) and which would be obsolete (derivatives traders). It wasn't just talk. My trading partner flew to Vermont to take a survivalist course. Sean Mallory bought a gun. And like many other paranoid Wall Street traders, I withdrew a chunk of money from the bank so that if things got bad, I would have cash on hand.

That day I walked down to the nearest Bank of America branch. When I asked the teller for $7,000, she asked me what it was for. I immediately felt guilty. If the world collapsed, I only wanted to save myself.

"Vegas," I said.

On the way back to work I stopped to pick up the usual lottery tickets for the guys at Pateras. Whenever the Mega Millions jackpot got above $100 million, we'd buy four tickets, with the potential winnings to be split between us. Sang Kim, a distressed-loan trading specialist (also obsolete in a Mad Max scenario), was about as senior as me. The other two guys were a few years younger and earned less, but their career paths stretched safely in front of them. They, too, would be rich.

We loved buying lottery tickets, because we got to spend the rest of the day talking about what we'd do with the money. The first thing, we all agreed, was quit. While Pateras was a dream job, it was still a job. We all woke up to the screech of an alarm clock, we all spent more time at work than we did with people we loved, and we all resented our bosses.

We talked about what we'd do when we quit, the houses

we'd buy in the Bahamas, or Jackson Hole, or Charleston. But it wasn't the houses we cared about—it was what life would look like when we were living in them, doing whatever we wanted to do. What we were really talking about was freedom.

Each time we bought lottery tickets, one issue would be hotly debated. *When* would we leave? What if we won the lottery in October? Some of us said we'd leave immediately, but others said that they would wait four months to receive their yearly bonus from Pateras. "Let's not forget," I sometimes said, "that even if you are a multimillionaire, one million dollars is a lot of money." We'd argue back and forth, and then someone would make a joke about high-class problems, and how pissed the rest of the world would be if four hedge fund guys won a $100-million jackpot. We'd laugh and then go back to talking about what we would do with the money.

That afternoon I went into an investment meeting with four people and Eldrick, four lottery tickets and a thick wad of hundreds in my front left pocket. The topic of discussion was the beaten down bonds of a struggling media company. As the meeting wound down, we started discussing the new financial regulations being discussed in Congress, which would be very restrictive to hedge funds. Everyone in the room thought they were a bad idea.

"But don't you think," I said, "the regulations make sense for the system as a whole?"

Eldrick shot me a withering glare. In a measured tone he said, "I don't have the brain capacity to think about the system as a whole, Sam. All I'm concerned with is how it affects us and our business."

He looked scared. That year, I would undoubtedly make millions—Eldrick would make *hundreds* of millions. But when I saw the expression on his face, I realized that the only difference between Eldrick and me was twenty years and a billion dollars. We were both afraid and were toiling under the delusion that the next million—or, in his case, hundred million—would make us feel safe. I chuckled as I ran my hand over the Benjamin Franklins in my pocket. *I'm pretty sure that this won't keep me safe if civilization as we know it ends.*

CHAPTER 33

Fear, Love, and a Billion Dollars

◻

The next morning when I walked into the office kitchen to pour myself a cup of coffee, I saw Jake Delancey, a shrewd analyst and one of the more powerful people at the firm, at the counter, making himself a protein shake. He nodded.

"Morning, Sam," he said.

"Morning, Jake."

"You look tired," he said. "You get laid last night?"

I can only imagine what my face looked like. No, I hadn't been laid. It had, ahem, been a while. And no, I didn't want to be asked that by a senior guy in the firm. I was sick and tired of what passed for conversation on Wall Street.

"No," I said.

"Too bad," he said. "When I was your age, I killed it. Like shooting fish in a barrel."

I tried to fake a smile—Jake would have a say about the size of my bonus—but I'm sure I betrayed some of my annoyance.

"It's never been that easy for me," I said, and walked out with my cup of coffee.

That comment was only the beginning of what would turn out to be a very long day with senior people at Pateras Capital.

Earlier that summer, Peter Conroy, one of the two billionaire founders, had announced a series of staff dinners. Each Wednesday, Peter would take eight analysts and traders out, and over the course of a meal he would share his knowledge of specific industries and his contacts with the team. That night was my dinner. I was dreading it.

Peter Conroy was the apotheosis of a thousand liberal nightmares. He brought his own wine to dinner parties so he wouldn't have to taste inferior swill. He mentioned the names of his rich and powerful friends two to three times a conversation. He seemed to believe that his vast wealth was the direct result of his innate superiority.

I'd started to see Peter as emblematic of Wall Street's hypocrisy. But Peter had something I wanted, had always wanted. Peter was as high as it got on Wall Street. When Peter walked into a room, conversation stopped. He became the center of the room. People listened eagerly to his stories, laughed at his jokes, orbited around him. He was The Man.

But being in Peter's presence could be grueling. He was always asserting his dominance—he was the boss; we were mere underlings. It was like spending time with Napoleon.

That night, Peter sat at the head of the table and opened the discussion with a story about how before everyone arrived, the waiter came in and saw him sitting at the head of the table and had commented that he must be the boss, because he clearly was comfortable in a leadership position. Then Peter started around the table, asking each analyst or trader about their sectors and telling them what he knew about those industries.

I had endured hundreds of business dinners with people I didn't like—that was just part of the job—but this dinner was different. Peter would focus his attention on one person, and while he was talking, the other traders and analysts would sit quietly and listen. But every few seconds, one of them would glance toward me and almost imperceptibly widen their eyes, as if to say wordlessly, *How ridiculous is this?*

I started to think about what Peter really had. He definitely had power. Our presence and our closed mouths attested to that. The moment Peter turned his attention to someone new, that person would bloom under his gaze. Suddenly they'd smile, listen attentively, and nod. It was like watching a table full of puppets. I did the same when Peter's attention was on me.

But Peter's power came from his position. It came from his wallet. I wasn't here because I admired Peter's character. As I watched him cut into his $50 steak, I realized how gravely I'd miscalculated. I didn't want what Peter had. I didn't want to be respected for the size of my wallet, or the name of the firm on my business card. I wanted to be respected for my character, for some real contribution.

Suddenly, I saw in full clarity the structure of the fantasy I had toiled under my whole life. If I achieved enough, made enough money, then someday in the future I would no longer be afraid and would get all the love I craved. That's what I thought a billion dollars would get me. But I had seen the fear in Eldrick's eyes, and that night, surrounded by sycophants, Peter looked to me like the loneliest person in the world. Somewhere inside of him, I think he knew that.

I didn't know whether Peter was seeking the same thing I was, but I could see that he was still seeking. And that went against my whole fantasy of becoming a billionaire. I'd thought that once I became a billionaire, I could finally rest. But that hadn't proved true for Eldrick and Peter. And that meant it wasn't about the money.

I had already known that, I realized; that was why the debate about whether it made sense to work for four or five months *after* winning the lottery to secure the next year's bonus had seemed reasonable. Winning the lottery wasn't going to be enough.

In a very real sense, with over a million dollars in the bank, I had *already* won the lottery. At that moment it finally hit me that I already had enough to do whatever it was I wanted to do. Freedom wasn't about the money. It was a state of mind. Yes, a million dollars in the bank helps. A lot. But there are plenty of people with much more who are prisoners in their own lives. All my life I'd felt handcuffed to a treadmill, sure that the next achievement or bonus would allow me to stop running. Now I realized the keys to the handcuffs had been in my pocket, not Peter's, the whole time.

After dinner, the analysts and traders milled about on the sidewalk, waiting for a cab and talking about how painful the dinner was. An analyst sidled up to me and said, "Wow, Sam, I'm impressed. You didn't smile at one of Peter's bad jokes." I felt a flash of pride, but it quickly faded. When Peter's attention was on me, I had sucked up like all the rest.

Over the remaining few months of that year, I met Marshall for coffee a dozen times. He had taken a job running trading for a boutique investment firm that was looking to grow into a power player.

Marshall and I would meet at a Starbucks between our two offices, and I would mostly talk about work at Pateras. When I first mentioned to Marshall that I was thinking about leaving, he was aghast.

"Sam," he said, "I am not sure you fully understand the position you are in."

I laughed. "Sure I do, Marshall," I said. "That's what makes this so hard."

"Look," Marshall said. "You are the head distressed trader at one of the biggest hedge funds in the world. You are on the cusp of one of the great careers on Wall Street. If you keep your Pateras seat for two or three more years, investors will be calling you to start your own hedge fund."

I smiled. Marshall had a tendency toward the dramatic, but his pronouncement was nice to hear.

"That's the thing, Marshall," I said. "It's always two years out. Everything I've ever wanted has been two years out. First I wanted to be a trader, then I wanted to be a CDS trader, then I wanted to be a distressed trader, now I'm *at* a hedge fund, and what I want is to *run my own* hedge fund. And to do it, I need to work in a place I don't much like, doing work that doesn't bring any value to the world."

Marshall was waiting for his turn to speak what for him was gospel. "In a few years *you* can be the boss and hire whoever you want. And you can use the money to do whatever you really want to do."

This had been Marshall's strategy, and it seemed a good one. He owned houses in Sun Valley and Charleston. He belonged to Winged Foot and Kiowa, two of the most prestigious country clubs in the nation. He owned two of the most popular restaurants in Charleston, and bars in Tribeca and East Hampton. He'd used his money to create the kind of world he wanted to live in, restaurants and bars where everyone knew his name.

I wanted that, too. Over the years my younger brother Daniel had become an accomplished chef, and we often talked about starting a restaurant together. There were other things I wanted to do—start a social enterprise, build an affordable alcohol and drug rehab center—and Marshall knew that, too.

"Whatever good things you want to do in the world will only be helped by the potentially hundreds of millions of dollars you can make," he said.

Marshall had just enunciated my biggest fear about leaving. I had put myself into a position that few people in the world experience. I had a real shot at attaining unimaginable wealth. I could use that money to do a lot of good. But there was something disconnected about having millions in the bank and going to work every day with the sole purpose of accumulating *more*. It reminded me of the way I used to drink. The way I used to eat. Making money just to give it away seemed like some form of financial bulimia.

One day in late summer, I emerged from a subway station at Union Square and ran into an old friend from college. Tara, a glowing redhead, had dated my friend Francisco in college, and we'd all spent many nights together. I'd lost touch with her over the years.

"How have you been?" I asked, after we had stepped to the sidewalk.

She told me about graduate school, a romance that had blossomed into marriage, about buying a house.

"And you?" she asked.

I stood looking at her while I searched for words. The last few years of my life had been an epic struggle, a knight's quest. But Tara didn't know Wall Street. She wouldn't understand what it meant to be the head distressed trader at Pateras. I could tell her I was up hundreds of millions of dollars, by far my best year ever, but that seemed a little gauche. I realized that all the drama in my life over the past eight years could be reduced to a single word.

"Work," I said.

I looked up at Tara and found her looking at me quizzically.

"Sorry," I said, and laughed. "I was having a moment."

"You okay?" she asked.

"Yeah," I said. "I am."

"Were you thinking about Sloane?" she asked.

I looked at her, surprised. It had been months since I thought about Sloane Taylor.

"No," I said.

"Oh," said Tara. "I thought you might be. I have been wondering how you were taking the news."

"What news?" I asked.

"Sloane is getting married," Tara said.

CHAPTER 34

Peter Luger's

□

S loane Taylor is getting married. My muscles tensed, my stomach clenched. I waited for the inevitable wave of heartache to return.

Nothing happened.

I didn't feel *anything*. I took a cautious breath. Then another. The pain I had so long imagined did not appear. It'd been years since I last saw Sloane and months since I even thought about her. Sloane had been dating an up-and-coming Hollywood producer, and now she was marrying him. I thought I'd be envious, but I wasn't.

I'd carried around the fantasy of Sloane, the perfect woman, the woman who would make me whole. But I didn't want to chase fantasies anymore. I wanted something real. Someone imperfect who I truly loved, who would love me—the real me, the messy, insecure, damaged, transcendent, sober man I'd become—in return. If Sloane wasn't interested in me—*and by now*, I thought with a chuckle, *it's pretty clear she wasn't*—then I didn't want to be with her, either.

My relationship with women had already changed. It had been almost two years since I stopped looking at porn. Several months after I quit, I started having an easier time with women than I ever had before. I'm not sure if it was because they sensed I was no longer trying to steal from them, or whether I just gave off a healthier energy. Or because I was a little older and a little richer. Whatever it was, I became attractive to women in the way I'd always wanted. For the first time in my life, lots of women were interested in me. I dated women at work, friends of friends, my yoga teacher, a woman I met on the street. I had a string of short, casual relationships with women I liked but did not love.

I'd always thought that dating and sleeping with tons of women would make me happy. When I finally experienced that, it was the same as all the other fantasies: the reality wasn't nearly as satisfying as what I'd imagined. I'd meet a woman and thrill at taking her home, but when it was over I was left with a woman in my bed whom I wasn't sure I wanted there. As soon as the sex was over, I often just wanted to be alone.

I liked sex, and I liked sex with different women, but in the end it left me more lonely and disconnected than before. I decided to stop.

Several months passed, and for the first time in my life I wasn't focused on luring in women. It wasn't that I didn't want a relationship—I did. But now I was willing to wait patiently until I found a woman I cared about.

I didn't have to wait long.

I'd moved to a modest attic apartment in Brooklyn Heights, and Ben came to stay with me for the summer. It was 2009, and he had just graduated from Harvard's Kennedy School, where he'd been elected student body president, and was about to start Harvard Law School. Instead of returning to consulting or going into corporate law, he planned to do poverty law, providing legal services to those who couldn't afford it. Toward the end of summer, he hosted a brunch at my apartment. He invited some college friends over and cooked coconut pancakes.

I'd been out all morning and arrived late. I pushed the door to my apartment open and froze. It was as if all the lights in the room were off except the ones around the woman standing in the middle of the room. She was tall, with long brown hair, the brightest smile I had ever seen, and deep blue eyes.

It was Kirsten Thompson, the girl I'd made out with when I'd gone to visit Ben at Cornell thirteen years earlier. I hadn't seen her since.

Her face looked the same, but her hair was now long and straight, and curled at the ends. She carried herself with confidence, grace. She was smiling without flirting. Warm without being effusive. She was stunning. I couldn't take my eyes off her.

I walked up to her and introduced myself, and she remembered me. I tried to think of interesting things to say so she would keep talking to me. I asked her about her life since we last saw each other, and she told me her story.

After Cornell she'd come to New York to work for J.P. Morgan. The office was a block from the World Trade Center, and her first day on Wall Street had been September 11, 2001. She was in the lobby when the first tower went down, and when smoke and debris exploded past the window she was standing next to, she ran for her life. As she ran, she saw a portly middle-aged man running alongside her, clutching his briefcase. She noticed how tightly he held onto it. *I don't want that to be me*, she thought.

She quit her job at J.P. Morgan. Lots of people said she was crazy to leave such a lucrative career. But she had seen what she had seen and didn't want a life dedicated to the security of money. She didn't want to be running for her life, clutching her briefcase.

She went back to school to become a doctor. For two years she worked full-time in a medical lab and took premed courses, waking at 5:00 a.m. to study for three hours before work. Then she applied to medical school and was accepted. Now, she was about to graduate. She was going to be a surgeon.

There were a few moments where we stopped talking and just looked at each other awkwardly, and then both started laughing.

At noon everyone started to leave, and Ben called me over to help him wash dishes. When I looked up, I saw Kirsten about to walk out the door. She was all the way across the room, so when she smiled and waved at me, I just waved back.

After she left, I asked Ben about calling her. He had been friends with Kirsten since college, and even though he wasn't romantically interested in her, I knew that after what he and I had been through, I needed to talk to him before asking one of his close friends out on a date. We'd worked through our issues about Emma Ramsdale, but there was still some soreness. That conversation brought up some old issues, which we talked through, and then Ben gave me his blessing.

Kirsten agreed to meet me for coffee on a Sunday afternoon. That day I was meeting Marshall and a few Wall Street guys at Peter Luger's Steak House in Williamsburg for lunch, so I planned to eat and then walk three miles to a coffee shop in Park Slope to meet Kirsten.

Peter Luger's was my favorite restaurant in the world. It was old school: wooden tables, no tablecloths, career waiters. The clientele varied, from Wall Street traders to lower-middle-class families from the Bronx, from slick Italian guys taking their girlfriends out for dates to old couples from Coney Island celebrating their anniversaries.

The food was incredible. The meal started with thick sliced onions and tomatoes with heavy homemade blue-cheese dressing. Then, salty slabs of bacon that you needed a knife to cut. Next, sizzling, redolent lamb chops with au jus spooned over them. For dinner, huge porterhouses on family-size plates so hot that if you wanted your steak cooked a little more, you slapped it on the side of the plate with a snap and a sizzle, and a minute later it was browned. There were bowls of heavy-creamed spinach and German-spiced potatoes. I covered everything in Peter Luger's heavy, sweet steak sauce. It was the only restaurant in the world where I wouldn't eat the bread; the rolls were delicious, but everything else was so much better.

The best part of the meal was dessert, which at Peter Luger's was a two-course affair. First, the waiter would drop off a large bowl of "Schlag"—heavy, sweet, freshly whipped cream. He'd toss dozens of gold-foil-covered chocolate coins on the table. While you perused the dessert menu, you'd use the chocolate coins to scoop Schlag into your mouth. The dessert menu was all-American: hot-fudge sundaes, thick slabs of apple pie. I always ordered the pecan pie—easily the best I'd ever had. It was so sweet it made your teeth chatter.

But Peter Luger's wasn't my favorite place in the world because of the food. It was my favorite place in the world because I ate there with Marshall. He'd been eating at Peter Luger's at least once a month for twenty years—he no longer needed a reservation. He started bringing me when I was a junior trader. I was a little surprised when he invited me. Marshall had so many friends that the faces at the table were almost always new; Marshall could assemble a dozen or more people at Peter Luger's for a late Sunday lunch with a few phone calls and an hour's notice. His crowd was hard drinking and loud, and I was sober and shy. But Marshall invited me anyway.

Marshall treated me like I wished my father had. He never let me pay for anything. He seemed happy I was there, even when I didn't say a word. And I trusted him. I knew unequivocally that Marshall was on my side, even though we were different in many respects. Marshall liked nothing more than a boozy dinner and a late night at a bar; I liked quiet dinners and nights alone. People would sometimes ask me how it was that Marshall and I were so close, even though our social lives were so different. "I don't know," I'd say. All I knew was that Marshall loved me unconditionally.

I talked to Marshall about leaving Wall Street more than anyone, and sometimes he would really *get* it. He would lean in toward me, listening intently, while I talked about how I no longer believed being rich would make me happy or that making money was a sufficient purpose for my life. He would say things like, "By God, Sam, you really don't compromise, do you?" and "Your work with Linda seems to have given you a much deeper way of looking at the world." But then he'd start talking about how things would be different for him when *the next* trading desk became a market leader, despite the fact that he had already run three different number one trading desks.

He'd been in the game too long to agree with me. Marshall was forty-five and had worked harder than anyone I knew. He spent his life on trading floors, in Michelin-starred restaurants and old New York bars like P. J. Clarke's, and usually returned home alone, or, if he was lucky, with a stranger he'd met at the bar. He had the biggest heart of any man I ever knew, but he had never married. My surrogate father might never become a real father. He had committed his life to the fulfillment of a fantasy I was now calling false.

I loved Marshall. I wasn't angry or disappointed with him—just the opposite. I planned to spend the rest of my life honoring him for what he'd done for me. That day, at Peter Luger's, Marshall had a new date with him, an attractive blond woman, ten or fifteen years younger, with the glazed-eye look of a woman three drinks into numbing herself to endure a night with a man she is with for reasons other than love. As usual, Marshall was in the midst of telling a story, and the whole table was captivated. Instead of listening, I watched his face. I looked at the red, puffy skin drooping exhaustedly from his cheeks, the visible consequence of five thousand consecutive restaurant dinners. And I looked at his eyes, already glazed from too much food and drink, and knew that on this next step of my life I couldn't look to Marshall for guidance. Navigating Wall Street, Marshall was my guy; leaving Wall Street, I was on my own.

At the end of the meal, we stood up from the table and walked through the bar to the front door. Marshall let the rest of the party go ahead of us so we could have a private word.

"How are you doing, buddy?" he asked. "Your thoughts seem elsewhere."

I smiled at him. "They are. Happens a lot these days."

"I'm proud of you," he said. "It takes courage to do what you are thinking about doing. I may not agree with it, but I admire it. I only wish you had a plan for once you leave."

We stood there silently. This would indeed all be easier if I had a new profession to dive into after leaving Wall Street. But I didn't. All I knew was that I needed out. I wanted an adventure.

I was scared. When I'd tell Wall Street guys I was thinking about leaving the business, the number one question they'd ask is, "How will you fill your time?" I understood the fear behind that question. It was scary to fathom days, weeks, and months where I didn't *have* to be somewhere, didn't have someone telling me what to do. One of the most terrifying passages I ever read was Thoreau writing about how sometimes he would spend an entire day sitting in his doorway, watching a field. *But what*, I wanted to scream, *did you DO all day?* Part of me realized the absurdity of fearing boredom from a life where I got to choose exactly what I did each day—I was afraid of the very thing I most wanted.

In *Netherland*, Joseph O'Neill wrote that one of the great consolations of work is its abbreviation of the world's space. I think he meant that at work, you know where you stand. Working in a successful hedge fund, with rich, successful people around me, I knew that, by the standards of the world, I was a success. Sometimes I would have the bizarre experience of reading about a rich finance guy in the paper and for a moment envying his life and success before remembering that I had reached the exact same success, and it had left me feeling empty. Now I was beginning to create my own definition of success.

And what if I was *wrong*? What if this whole plan to leave Wall Street was, as Marshall seemed to think, a well-meaning but adolescent process I had to go through that would ultimately lead me back to the sage realization that financial success was indeed what life was really about? If I stepped off the track, the race would go on. Each year, guys would make huge bonuses, get promoted, start new hedge funds. And I was proposing to do . . . nothing?

Since I could remember, I felt threatened by other people's success. Now, the entire world might pull past me. Guys I had left in the dust, like that trader in Vegas who had chanted, "Thirty-five sticks! I'm up thirty-five sticks!" would outearn me in a year or two. How would it feel to read newspaper articles in twenty years about guys I had started with on Wall Street who were now CEOs of investment banks or billionaire hedge fund managers?

It seemed safer to play by the rules I had always played by. What if I left Wall Street, and the rest of my life amounted to nothing? I was afraid that the infinite world would open up before me, and I would disappear into its terrifying maw. I believed that since I didn't know what was coming, then nothing might.

Marshall and I stood quietly for a second longer, lost in our own diverging thoughts. I was glad he was next to me. *The difference between Marshall and my dad is that if I step away from Marshall's world, I know he will still have my back.* I loved him for that.

"So you are going to see Kirsten now, huh?" Marshall said. "She sounds like an amazing woman."

I nodded, excited. I hugged Marshall, endured a round of handshakes, and then walked out into the brisk fall day.

As I walked to Park Slope from Williamsburg, I thought about what had happened in the thirteen years since Kirsten and I first met. I was an almost completely different person. I hoped she liked who I had become.

I was thirty minutes early, and when she finally walked into the coffee shop, she was even more beautiful than I remembered from a few weeks before.

This time she asked me about my life, and I told her I was thinking about leaving Wall Street. She told me that when she left J.P. Morgan, they had her talk to six or seven different people and each one was supposed to convince her to stay. When it became clear her mind was made up, each one started telling her about how they wanted to do something else with their lives.

One woman told her she wished her career involved helping people. A senior executive told her he had been trying to leave for a decade but year after year failed to muster the courage. The last guy she talked to said he'd never been happy on Wall Street, but he couldn't leave, because he felt compelled to maintain his family's lifestyle.

Even on Wall Street people live lives of quiet desperation.

It wasn't that Kirsten had it all figured out. She wasn't smug about being a doctor instead of an investment banker. She, too, struggled with feeling inadequate. Underneath the successful doctor was a shy, sometimes socially awkward

247

woman. I was glad for that. I stared at her in that coffee shop and thought that I could spend my life with this woman. I wondered if someday she might love me.

After coffee, we walked around Park Slope in a light rain for hours. We went into a chocolate store and had dessert. Afterward, I kissed her on the cheek and left and felt like something important had happened.

On our second date we went to a hole-in-the-wall Thai restaurant in Brooklyn and talked about our families. I told her about my dad, my alcohol and drug addiction, the crimes I'd committed—who I was, warts and all.

She started to talk about her family and quickly burst into tears. Her father was an alcoholic—he'd tried to keep his drinking hidden to protect her; she'd felt burdened by his secret. She told me about the beers in the garage, the hospital visits. She said my openness about my family, and myself, made her feel safe to talk about hers. She told me about siblings who'd struggled with drugs and crime. When she was finished talking, she looked vulnerable and exposed. I leaned over and kissed her cheek.

We both had masks. But we seemed ready to be honest with each other. Within a few dates, I'd connected with Kirsten on a deeper level than I had with any of my past girlfriends.

One night Kirsten and I went to dinner at a small café in my neighborhood, and from there we walked by a quiet neighborhood park. I pulled her to me and kissed her and remembered what her mouth felt like thirteen years before.

I was still scared of really letting someone see the real me. I was also afraid of what kind of husband I'd be. I worried that no matter how much work I did, I'd inevitably end up like my dad.

Kirsten and I were both gentle with each other from the start, as if we understood that something important was possible between us but that it was fragile. A few weeks later,

I dreamed Kirsten and I were riding in a horse-drawn carriage. She was wearing a white hat and a white dress. We were coming home from our wedding. It was an incredibly corny dream. I was embarrassed I'd even had it. When I told Kirsten, she burst into tears.

CHAPTER 35

Hear It in the Deep

◻

The Pateras Christmas party that year was held at the Metropolitan Club, one of the most elite private clubs in New York. Jacket and tie were required, and the cocktail hour was held in a jaw-dropping room with fifty-foot ceilings, million-dollar chandeliers, and marble floors. New York wealth and power made manifest.

I stood in a circle with the other traders, laughing and joking. I'd wanted to belong to a group my whole life, and now I did. We spent more time together than we did with our families. But another part of me saw that standing in a group of Wall Street guys can be the loneliest place in the world. What passes for conversation is a series of insults—*Great sweater, fuckface. Nice one, d-bag*—and comments about the waitress's ass.

It wasn't just the shallow conversation. It was the whole shallow career. I'd been mulling over a famous Bloomberg message that had been sent out by a Goldman trader to the entire market. The subject line read, "Size Does Matter"; the message said that he'd buy or sell $5 billion worth of an index of derivatives in a single phone call. It was the largest index market in history.

Taking a situation to its extreme can illuminate an otherwise obscured absurdity. *Why would anyone need to trade $5 billion* *in derivatives at a single moment?* The infrastructure, brain-power, and expertise needed to facilitate trades like that were *way* more costly than the benefits to the world. I was standing with a group of very intelligent people, and we were expending enormous amounts of energy developing sophisticated levels of expertise. But we were not building anything or creating anything of value. I knew hundreds of derivatives traders. I was a derivatives expert. And it occurred to me that the world would hardly change at all if credit derivatives ceased to exist. I'd become an expert in a profession that wasn't worth a damn.

I'd come to Wall Street for validation. I believed my value was in achievement, that achievement was conferred by institutions and rendered in money. I'd joined an army of bright young men and women dressed in business-casual uniforms, streaming into the service of massive corporations without any sense of why we'd chosen to dedicate our lives to further enriching the already rich, except that we needed proof that we were valuable, because at heart we didn't really believe we were.

One of the things I most loved about Wall Street when I first started was how connected I felt; I was paid to understand what was going on in the world. I actually had a reason to read the *Economist*.

Standing with the traders that night, I saw how disconnected we really were. We talked about people's lives as if they were variables in an equation. As if the most important thing about what was happening in the world was whether it would make stocks go up or down. Reading the newspaper had become like studying a chessboard—people were pawns in a trillion-dollar chess game.

What I'd mistaken for a connected life was a life lived inside a glass bubble. I sat safely ensconced in a Manhattan skyscraper, looking down at the world, judging it and making my bets so that I could accumulate more money.

And Sean had bought a *gun*. My withdrawing $7,000, El-drick's obsessive accumulation, and Sean buying a gun were all the same thing. The bottom line for us meant protecting our wealth.

Our obsessive accumulation of money had led to the widest inequality in centuries. Our hoarding had left millions of people unemployed, starving, and marginalized. Prison populations were swelling; families were starving. Our greed was the source of that poverty. We were the source of that marginalization.

I'd recently finished Taylor Branch's three-part series about Dr. King and the civil rights movement. I'd read about the Freedom Riders, civil rights activists in the '60s who rode interstate buses into the segregated South to test whether the recent Supreme Court ruling abolishing segregation was being upheld. I'd held my breath as the buses pulled into the Birmingham bus station, into a crowd of three thousand armed, screaming bigots. The Freedom Riders looked out the windows to see the furious mob wielding tire irons, bicycle chains, iron pipes, and guns. They opened the door and filed out. They walked *into* the mob. To take the vicious beating they knew was coming. And it came.

That image had seared into my mind. I told myself that if I were alive in the '60s, I would have been on that bus. What *bullshit*. There were countless injustices out there—rampant poverty, a porn and sexual assault epidemic, swelling prison populations, an obesity crisis—and I wasn't doing a thing about them. If I'd lived in the '60s, I would not have been on those buses with the Freedom Riders. I would have been betting on which companies would benefit from the civil rights movement. I would have been long the stocks and bonds of taxi companies and hospitals during the Rosa Parks bus strike, and I would have been short the department stores that were being boycotted. My words would have been on the side of the civil rights activists, but my actions would have been on the side of enriching myself.

I looked up at my colleagues and realized that I'd been lost in thought for the last several minutes, and no one had even noticed.

We had a special musical guest that night. Gavin DeGraw was a Grammy-winning musician. He was my age, and while I only knew a few of his songs, my sister was a devout fan. She'd shrieked when I told her Gavin was performing at my holiday party.

When I got to the table, Gavin's placard was next to mine. When he arrived, I shook his hand and told him my sister was a huge fan. That was the last thing I said to him the whole night. My teeth clamped; my tongue tied. I sat at the table, listening to Gavin talk about his music. I tried to will myself to participate in the conversation. Something held me back, as if my jaw had been wired shut.

In a flash, I saw myself in this opulent room, a pale-white, suit-wearing millionaire sitting amongst other pale-white, suit-wearing millionaires.

I realized how Gavin must see me. I wanted to pull him aside and tell him that I was different than all these Wall Street guys. But I realized how hollow that would sound. Where I stood was more important than what I said.

A few minutes later Gavin went onstage. He tested the piano and guitar and made a joke about feeling like a fish out of water. The crowd sat there, stiff in their chairs, with their linen tablecloths and silver and three wineglasses, and watched him. After each song they clapped perfunctorily. I watched, rapt, as he lost himself in the music.

In January, Kirsten and I sat in canvas chairs on a Santa Monica beach, watching the waves, waiting for sunset.

"How are you feeling?" I asked.

"I'm scared," she said.

"I'm scared, too," I said.

We had been dating for only three months, and some big decisions were upon us. I would receive my bonus in a couple weeks. Kirsten would graduate from medical school in the spring, and she was starting the process of choosing where to do her residency, a five-year postgraduate training program required of new doctors. We had come to California to talk about the future.

A few months before I met Kirsten, I asked a friend of mine about how he came to ask his wife to marry him. He said when he met her, he just knew. "When you meet the woman who will be your wife, Sam," he said, "you will just know."

I had doubted him, because relationships had never been like that for me. With girlfriends I was always keeping score in my head—a list of pros and cons—as if someday I would render a deciding verdict and the matter would be settled. But I was forever plagued with doubts and reservations, and I'd come to believe that that was what relationships were like.

With Kirsten, I learned that my friend had been right. I just knew. It hadn't happened at the snap of a finger. I had too many defense mechanisms still active from a childhood of seeing relationships modeled as a lifelong cage match. But I kept walking through those fears until one day I simply knew that this was the woman I wanted to be with.

Here we were, three months into our relationship, deciding where to spend the next five years. Kirsten would go through a process called the Match, where medical school graduates are paired with residency programs where they will work for the next five years. Kirsten had interviewed at eighteen programs, in New York, DC, Philadelphia, and Los Angeles, and would be submitting her list in a few weeks.

Kirsten loved New York. But I was ready to leave. The thought of quitting Wall Street but still being around all the money and ambition seemed overwhelming.

There were so many unknowns. We sat there in silence

and watched the ocean, the same ocean I had fallen into at camp when I was a kid and learned in that one terrifying moment that I had to fight in order to survive. As the sun touched the water, and pinks and peaches exploded over the cloud-speckled sky, I watched the waves roll in. My eyes fastened on a single wave in the distance. First, it was a swell, then it became a peak, and finally it crested over into an explosion of white water, which then dissipated as the wave trudged onward toward the land, finally turning into little more than a ripple that then, exhausted, spilled itself onto the sand in one last gasp toward the destination it had been rushing toward for months, across hundreds of thousands of miles. The water finally came to a point, as far up the sand as it was destined to go. Some of it sank into the wet sand. Some was picked up by a boy with a bucket, and the rest turned back whence it came, becoming one with the next wave. As I looked out past that next wave, I saw a line of waves as far as the eye could see, all unique and all carrying the history of a great journey within them and yet all, in some sense, the same. I realized that my life was like that single wave, that I was on a great journey, over great distances, but at the end what had happened to the wave would happen to me.

Suddenly I knew that none of the questions I had mattered. It didn't matter whether I got richer or not, whether we lived in New York or LA, or even Philadelphia. It didn't matter, because there was no correct destination.

I was calmer than I'd ever been in my entire life. Because I finally understood that I could stop trying to prove myself, stop trying to make it to the top. I finally understood that I was enough . . . had always been . . .

CHAPTER 36

The Bright Light
of the Afternoon

◻

Two weeks later, on a Friday, my bonus hit my bank account. I planned to wait a week and then resign. That afternoon, I noticed that Sean, Eldrick, and Peter were engaged in intense conversation in Eldrick's glass office. A few minutes later, Sean walked out and went into his office. Peter and Eldrick continued talking. After a half hour, they both emerged and stood near my desk. Sean came out of his office. Peter cleared his throat.

"Everyone, please come over here," he said.

He waited till everyone was gathered around the trading desk. "We have an announcement," said Peter. "Sean Mallory resigned today and will be leaving the firm next month."

Boom.

I was one of five senior traders on the desk. With Sean gone, Derek and I would be the leading candidates to run trading. Peter and Eldrick thanked Sean for his contribution; there was a round of applause. Sean went back into his office, and the crowd dissipated. A few seconds later, I received a message from Sean asking me to go back there. I stepped into his office and closed the door behind me.

"Wow," I said. "Congratulations."

"Thank you," he said. He looked energized.

We were both quiet for a second. Then I said, "I'm leaving, too."

His head snapped toward me.

"Why? Don't you realize how good for you this is?" he said.

"I don't know, Sean," I said. "I see the path you took. And I see that some form of it is open to me now. But I'm not willing to trade years of my life for money. I mean, what happens if you die next year? What then?"

He laughed. "If I die next year," he said, "then it's been a bad trade. But I don't think I will, and I've made a boatload of money."

Sean's comment stung. There was a clause in my Pateras contract that said if I left I'd have to leave half this year's bonus—$1.8 million—on the table. It would be a lot easier to leave Wall Street with a fortune like Sean's.

We were quiet a moment. "Look," Sean said. "I know you've been bummed out about pay. I feel like I let you down."

I'd never heard him say anything like that. I was surprised at his accountability.

"You did let me down," I said. "You thought I was getting underpaid, and you didn't stand up for me." My throat was thick with emotion.

Sean didn't respond.

I turned to leave.

"You should really think about staying," Sean said, from over my shoulder. "Eldrick talks about you as one of the top three guys in the firm that he listens to. He respects you. If you have any doubt about leaving, you should push Eldrick and Peter to pay you more. I'm sure they'd be willing to."

Sean's leaving created a huge opportunity for me. A $3.6-million bonus would be nothing compared to what Pateras might pay me next year, with Sean gone. Still, I was determined to leave—I didn't want to be a part of this selfish, arrogant culture any longer.

That Wednesday, I got an e-mail from Eldrick saying he wanted to meet with me to discuss my future at Pateras, to address any concerns I might have, and to let me know what a valued employee I was.

The next day I sat down with Eldrick and listened as he complimented my investing. He said that I could spot trends before they were obvious, that I consistently had a unique opinion on the world, which led to smart, creative investments. Listening to him, I felt proud.

Eldrick asked me about myself. I told him I wanted to help people, to make a real contribution to society.

He started telling me about his philanthropic activities. He said he gave money anonymously, because he wasn't in it for the credit. I wondered if he realized the irony of *telling* someone that he donates money anonymously. But I was also impressed.

The next morning, Peter came by my desk and asked to see me in a conference room. "Sam," he began, "I wanted to talk with you and address any concerns you might have after Sean's resignation. I spoke with Eldrick yesterday and got the rundown, so I thought I'd tell you about my charitable ventures."

As Peter described his charitable giving, I grew angry. Peter and Eldrick had paid me less than I deserved. Now, with Sean gone, my value to them had grown. But instead of raising my bonus, they were trying to impress me with how socially conscious they were. But that was bullshit.

Suddenly, I realized I had leverage. Maybe there was a way I could leave Wall Street with even more money than I had, if I played my cards right.

That night, I told Kirsten I was going to negotiate for more money.

"But I thought you were leaving," she said.

"I am," I said. "But I might be able to leave with a few more million in the bank."

"But you can't negotiate a higher bonus," she said, "and then resign right after."

"Why not?" I said, defensive. "I deserved a bigger bonus this year. They owe me."

She didn't say anything, but I could tell she was unconvinced. And the truth was, I could feel that there was something askew in my plan. But I wanted that money.

"You don't understand," I said to Kirsten. "This is a great opportunity."

The next day, I got up early and rode the subway to the office. At eight, when Peter and Eldrick arrived, I sent them both an e-mail asking to meet me in a conference room. I stood up from the trading desk, and walked to the corner conference room. It had floor-to-ceiling windows overlooking Central Park.

When we were all sitting down, I began.

"Thank you both for reaching out to me over the past few days. We covered several subjects. One that we only touched on was my compensation, and I'd like to address that now. It's important for me that I am passionate about what I am doing, and in order for that to happen, I need to know my compensation is in line with my contributions. I had a hugely profitable year this year. I think a bonus of eight million dollars would have been fair, and you came in well below that. I wanted to talk with you about raising this year's compensation up to that level."

I stopped talking. We all just sat there.

Eldrick spoke first. "Sam, obviously you were a big part of things this year. Your ideas were excellent. I agree you had a big impact."

I nodded.

"Wait a second," Peter said. "How did you get to eight million dollars?"

There was something about the tone of his voice. It reminded me of my dad. How Dad used to barrage me with questions whenever I asked for money.

"I don't intend to argue with you about the number," I said to Peter, irritated.

He held his hands up, miffed. "Argue? You brought up the number. I'm just asking how you came to it."

"Okay," I said tersely, leaning forward, and rattled off the big trades I'd made that year, all massively profitable, and how I'd been told that each year my percentage payout would go up, but it had, in fact, gone down.

Eldrick jumped in. "Yes, Sam, I agree you made big contributions. There were a lot of times you saw the trade before anyone else. I just wish we had known you were dissatisfied earlier."

"Well, I wanted to wait until my bonus check cleared," I said. "There was an inherent imbalance of power until I had the money that you owed me in my possession."

Peter looked like I had slapped him in the face. "We would never not pay a check because someone brought up an issue like this. We have fifteen years of reputation here, Sam. You need to be reasonable. You need to show us some faith."

All of a sudden, I was angrier than I'd ever been in my life. Not just at Peter, but at Eldrick, Sean, all the bosses that had ever underpaid me. Why couldn't they see what I was worth? Why did I always have to beg for more?

And then, suddenly, my anger grew in intensity, like a forest fire catching a gust. They were acting just like my dad—not giving me the money I deserved. I hadn't felt this much rage since I was a boy.

"I think, Peter, that it's *you* who needs to show some faith," I said, jabbing my finger at him. "Because what's missing here is *my trust in you*. I have been here two and a half years and I made you a ton of money. If we are to stay in business together, then I'm going to need to see more from you than I've seen so far."

He looked like it had been a long time since someone had spoken to him like that. He shook his head. "This is highly irregular," he said.

We sat there a moment. Then Peter said, "Well, if we do increase your bonus, a lot of it will be deferred"—which meant I wouldn't receive the money for two to three years. So that was the deal. I could get more money, but I'd have to stay. And I knew I wasn't willing to stay another year, no matter how much they paid.

I told them I was unwilling to accept deferred compensation. If they weren't willing to pay me the money now, I would walk.

They asked me to give them some time to think it over.

"What is your timeline?" I asked.

Peter snapped. "What is this timeline? Why do you want a timeline?"

"Every contract negotiation needs a timeline," I said.

Peter's face reddened. "Sam! You just threw all of this on our laps, and now you demand a timeline. You need to be reasonable! *Come on!*"

I had poked a bull. "I can be reasonable," I said.

Peter said, "Okay. Okay. Obviously we value your contribution."

I left work early that day, and when I came in the next morning, Sean called me into his office. "Do you want me to salvage this?" he started.

"What do you mean, salvage?" I asked.

"They are furious," he said. "You told them you don't trust them. You went in really aggressive. That was not the right way to handle things."

My heart sank. My bravado from the day before had faded, and now I was left with the disappointment of not getting what I'd asked for.

"Look, Sean," I said. "It's not my responsibility to manage their feelings. I said what I had to say. How they react is their business."

In the afternoon I got a call from Peter, who asked me to come downstairs to a small conference room. When I got there, I saw it was just Peter and the firm's head lawyer. Peter had a cold look on his face. He said, "Look, Sam, you are a really valued employee, but there are certain ways to handle things, and you came in very aggressively. You asked for eight million dollars. If we were going to give you anything, it would be deferred, which you said you don't want, so that leaves us here . . . We are not prepared to meet that number. So what do you want to do?"

There was nothing left for me to do except play out the hand I'd dealt. I looked into Peter's eyes defiantly. "I said exactly what I needed to say. If you are not going to meet my terms, then it's time that we part ways." I stood up.

"I'm sorry to hear that," Peter said. "I think you could make a lot of money here."

But money was no longer my primary goal. I looked down at Peter, and the lawyer who hadn't said a word, then walked out without shaking either of their hands.

I went back upstairs, grabbed my bag, and shook hands with the guys on my row. I heard Sean's phone ring, and he picked it up and then looked at me. I knew it was Peter calling to tell him I'd resigned. I looked at Sean and then looked away so he wouldn't see the disappointment on my face. Disappointment that he hadn't stood up for me. Disappointment that he hadn't been the father I had looked for in every boss I'd ever had. As I walked to the door leading off the trading floor, I saw Sean stand up, the phone pressed to his ear, watching me. I took one final look around the place that had embodied all the dreams I had ever had but that I had come to detest, and then I walked out the door, took the elevator down, and stepped into the bright light of the New York afternoon, with no idea what I was going to do with the rest of my life.

Good-bye to All That

○

S ix years have passed since I left Wall Street.
I remember waking up that first morning after I quit, feeling scared and alone, but also exhilarated. Never before had my options seemed so limitless. I had no idea what I would do, or where I would be next year, or even next week.

Ben and I went backpacking in Mexico. It was a style of travel I was unaccustomed to, carrying only one extra pair of clothes, sleeping in hostels, traveling by bus. It was grimy, hot, and exhausting, and I loved every minute of it. I realized that with only a few bucks and a decision, I could go anywhere in the world.

When I returned to New York a week later, I took a cab to Kirsten's apartment. When she opened the door she didn't say anything, just handed me an envelope. Inside was a single piece of paper, which read *University of Southern California, Surgical Residency Program*. We were moving to Los Angeles; I was going home.

But first, we were going to India, where Kirsten had secured a two-month internship at a hospital in Bangalore. I packed up my entire apartment and put it in storage, and left three weeks before she did, to travel alone through Europe. I saw Paris for the first time. I got lost in Seville. Standing alone on the prow of the ferry between Spain and Morocco, looking across the water at the giant Rock of Gibraltar, I felt so free and alive that I laughed out loud. In India, Kirsten and I hiked the Himalayas, spent a week on a houseboat in Kerala, saw the Taj Majal, and after we both caught vicious stomach bugs while sharing a tiny hotel room, got to know each other on a much more intimate level.

On our return, we moved to Los Angeles, where I started living the life of my dreams. Waking up without an alarm. Surfing nearly every day. Reading books by the dozen. Going to movies in the middle of the day. Sitting for hours at coffee shops. Making new friends, and living with Kirsten. It was amazing.

And yet after a while I felt like something was missing. I started volunteering at a shelter for homeless youths. I taught a writing class to high school girls in a group foster home. I started going into jails and juvenile detention centers to speak to the inmates about getting sober. I was searching for a purpose.

In 2013, three years after I left Wall Street, Kirsten and I watched a movie called *A Place at the Table*. It was about hunger in America—how, in the richest country in the world, millions of people, many of them children, don't know where their next meal is coming from.

What really blew my mind was the point the film made about the confluence of poverty and obesity. Poor families in America often live in food deserts, where little produce is available, and lots of fast food. They might skip one meal, but eat KFC at the next because that's all that's available, which is part of why the poorest Americans are the most obese.

That broke my heart. I remembered my childhood, how there was never enough money but too much violence, and how I'd turned to food to quell my fear and anxiety. But there had been plenty of grocery stores in my neighborhood. The thought of kids living just five miles from me who didn't know where their next meal was coming from, who were under deep emotional stress, and who couldn't stay healthy because there was no healthy food around—that just seemed too much, too hard. Kirsten and I decided to do something.

We founded Groceryships ("Scholarships for Groceries"), a nonprofit working at the intersection of poverty and obesity. Groceryships helps moms living in food deserts to get themselves and their families healthy. When a mom joins, she becomes part of a group of ten other moms. For six months, these moms meet weekly for two hours to learn about nutrition, healthy cooking, and practical skills about how to navigate an unhealthy environment. The meetings are structured as support groups—most of the two hours is spent talking about family, stress, and other emotional issues surrounding food. At each meeting, each family receives approximately $40 in fresh produce.

These group meetings aren't expert-led and didactic; they are peer-led, community based, and led by graduates of previous groups. People find out about Groceryships through word of mouth, and at our community center in South LA, applications pour in every day. In 2016, we will run thirty groups (three hundred moms), and our waiting list is over 150 names long.

I have been the executive director of Groceryships for three years. During the past year, I cofounded a new for-profit social enterprise called Everytable, and became its CEO. Everytable sells fresh, healthy, ready-to-eat meals that are affordable for all. We open storefronts in low-income neighborhoods, where we sell meals for approximately $3.50. In higher-income neighborhoods, our storefronts sell meals for $7, far less expensive than other healthy food options. This variable pricing model is a totally new concept, and there's a lot of excitement around our start-up company.

So, Wall Street trader to social entrepreneur, sinner to saint, everything is perfect, right?

Not exactly.

Several times over the past six years, I've gotten hit with a feeling of deep regret about all the money and connections I walked away from. For a few months, I'll feel a pit of fear in my stomach, wondering if I made the right decision. Boarding a plane, I'll feel consumed with envy of the first-class passengers comfortably sipping their complimentary champagne. I'll start fantasizing about how life will be better when I have a mansion in Malibu, or when I achieve my no-longer-secret dream of becoming president of the United States.

As a scared and lonely kid, I sponged up the power fantasies of our culture. And even now, after I have seen behind the curtain, the grooves of those neural pathways, formed during childhood, are so deep that sometimes I still believe the illusions they conjure.

It is so very hard to step away from the values of a culture.

But most of the time, I am just very grateful for my life. For six years, I haven't had a boss. I've created things— Groceryships, Everytable, a front-page *New York Times* OpEd piece, this book—that express who I am, and what I believe. My work is both challenging and meaningful, and I am proud of it.

*　　*　　*

Oh, and Kirsten and me?

We got married. We have a close, loving relationship. It isn't perfect. We have our issues, and sometimes we fight. We go to couples counseling. But we are happy and in love. Kirsten left surgery to become a psychiatrist, because she wanted to focus on emotional health and make time for being a mom.

In 2014 she gave birth to our first child, a girl named Eveline, who is the joy of our lives. Kirsten's father moved to Los Angeles, got sober, and is a rock of support for our young family.

And this is what I know:

I know that of all the things I do in my life, the most important will be how I love Kirsten and Eveline. There is no higher aim, for me, than to become the father I never had, and the kind of husband I never saw.

Hopefully, Eveline will know in the depth of her being that she is loved unconditionally and will pass that love on to her children, and they on to theirs, and so on and so on until that love is the only remaining vestige of our brief but meaningful lives.

Acknowledgments

◻

Writing and publishing this book has been an amazing journey, one that would not have started if not for Linda Redford, who suggested I write it, and supported me throughout the process. And, as you know by now, I would not be where I am today without Linda's guidance and teaching, and I will be forever grateful to her.

Thank you to my friend Joe Spiccia, a rock of support and a terrific and repeated reader. Thank you to Kurt Halvorson and Jerry Cudzil, who loved this book from the beginning, and whose friendship has meant more to me than they know.

Thank you to my agent, Sam Stoloff, who saw the potential in this book when few did. Thank you to Daniel Burgess at Scribner for buying this book. And thank you to John Glynn, my final editor at Scribner, for his vision and confidence in bringing this book to its right structure and full potential.

Thank you to Kristen Peterson, the first-ever reader of a draft of this book, without whose gentle encouragement I may never have become a writer.

Thank you to Jennie Nash, first my writing teacher at UCLA and then my independent editor for the last six years, whose honesty and incisive edits have made everything I've written better. I do not publish anything without her reading it first. To all writers or aspiring writers, I recommend Jennie.

Thank you to Carole Desanti, my earliest supporter in the world of publishing.

Thank you to the following readers for your insight, suggestions, and encouragement: Rob Robertson, Tristine Rainer, Michael Cassidy, Emily Wolf, Patrick Mulligan, Christina McDowell, Todd Rosenberg, Peter Huzzardi.

Thank you to Geneen Roth, whose late-inning suggestions made this a stronger book, and whose friendship and guidance I value deeply.

Thank you to Michael Meyer, whose kindness and generosity continue to amaze me, even today. Michael, I am grateful to have you in my life.

Thank you to my mom, who had the patience and love to work through everything with me, and who has become a treasured part of my life.

Thank you to my brother Daniel for his friendship and support.

Thank you to my sister, Julia, who brings so much laughter and joy into my life, and whom I love very deeply.

Thank you to my twin brother, Ben, for all the reads, and all the conversations, and for being my constant companion on this incredible journey.

And most of all thank you to my wife, Kirsten, for her patience, faith, and support. And to our daughter, Eveline, who shows me every day that I have not yet reached my capacity for love.